MW00479688

DON'T YOU DARE

Uncovering Lost Love

GAYLA TURNER

Print ISBN 978-1-09839-259-8

eBook ISBN 978-1-09839-260-4

Dedicated to Ruby (1896 – 1977)

PROLOGUE

I spent years researching my grandma's life and the clues she left behind. Yes, clues. She left just enough information that only someone who understood her secret life would be able to uncover the hidden story she left behind. It turned out to be a mystery I was uniquely qualified to solve.

As I examined her photos, I noticed how incredibly happy everyone looked. These weren't the typical stoic pictures taken in the early nineteen-hundreds. They were humorous and loving. However, if any of my grandma's photos had fallen into the wrong hands, she and everyone else involved could have been put into mental institutions, run out of town, or worse.

During my research it occurred to me that as wonderful as the photos were, the truth was tragic. This was as far as their relationship could ever go: all they could ever have were memories. If they dared to take photos, the pictures would quickly be destroyed to avoid the possibility of discovery. It struck me how brave my grandma was to keep her pictures for so many years; but then I've always been a believer that love makes us strong.

I often wonder if Grandma Ruby hoped that someday someone would find out about her secret life. Did she suspect it would be me?

ONE

There they were: the boxes. As soon as we walked into my Aunt Patty's living room, Mom looked at the two brown, medium-sized cardboard boxes stacked in the corner next to the avocado-green couch. My aunt lived closest to the nursing home, and after Grandma Ruby passed away on April 12, 1977, all of her belongings were transported to Aunt Patty's one-bedroom apartment in St Louis.

I was sixteen at the time, and I remember traveling with my mom from Los Angeles to St. Louis to attend Grandma's funeral. Mom told me we needed to stay a couple of extra days so she could sort out some of her mother's belongings. She claimed it wouldn't take too long, because Grandma didn't have anything of great value.

Mom walked across the living room and placed her hand lightly on the top box, as if silently saying hello to an old friend. Then she grimaced and quickly pulled it away. "I remember them being bigger. What do you suppose we should do with them?" she asked Aunt Patty, as she wiped dust from her fingertips.

My aunt must have expected that question. "I don't know what to do with them. I thought we'd go through Mother's other things first, and then decide what to do with her boxes."

I watched TV while the two of them negotiated their mother's belongings. Mom was right; the process was quick.

Then my mom looked in the direction of those boxes, still stacked neatly in the corner of the room. "Well?" she asked, her hands resting on her hips.

Aunt Patty shot back, "You can see I don't have any room here in this tiny apartment for another box, let alone two of them."

Mom's rebuttal was swift. "I couldn't possibly take them on the flight back home with us; they'd fall apart before we landed."

After another round of negotiations, Mom agreed to having the boxes shipped back to our home in California, but only if Aunt Patty paid the cost of freight.

✑⁘✑

Since 1921, Grandma Ruby had quietly moved those two boxes with her wherever she lived. Even after her husband left the family in 1939, she moved the boxes, along with her three children, to various boarding homes and apartments. From Amherst, Wisconsin, to Minneapolis; from Minneapolis to Assumption, Illinois; and a dozen other places after that. The last move for Grandma Ruby and her boxes was to a nursing home in St Louis in 1975. In 1977, at the age of 82, my grandmother passed away, never revealing their secret contents.

TWO

After Mom was diagnosed with dementia in 2009, my sister Janice and I would often drive from Southern California to Mom's place in Pahrump, Nevada. We tried convincing her to move closer to us and her grandchildren, but after living alone for the last twenty years she had no interest in being anywhere other than in a doublewide trailer in the middle of the desert.

Most people hated driving the long stretch of desert highway between Barstow and Pahrump, but I found the vast emptiness peaceful: no cars or people for almost one hundred miles. However, as Mom's dementia worsened, it seemed as if the highway stretched longer and longer with every trip. At times, it felt as if my car was on a treadmill and I was looking at the same mounds of sand and tumbleweeds for hours.

During our visits, my sister and I would often spend time reminiscing over the family photos Mom had collected through the years. We'd dig into the old department-store boxes with both hands and pull out a group of photos to look at. After she retired, Mom often told us she was going to organize the family photos and put them in albums someday, but we all knew that wasn't going to happen.

We'd laugh and share pictures and stories with Mom. She'd often laugh along with us, but I wasn't sure she really knew who or what we were talking about. At the time I thought we were doing it to help Mom recapture her stolen memories, but I now know Janice and I did it to recapture our own.

On one of my visits with Mom, I was looking for more photos to share when I noticed two medium-sized boxes stacked at the far end of her closet, marked 'Mother's old photos.' I was surprised—up to that point I thought I had seen every family picture many times over, but I had never seen these boxes. Or so I thought.

I suddenly felt like a twelve-year-old at Christmas; I couldn't wait to see what was inside. As I pulled them from the safety of my mother's closet, I could hear the brittle brown cardboard creaking in protest with every tug. A cloud of dust followed me as I placed them in the middle of my mom's living room.

When I opened the first box I could tell instantly that the pictures were like nothing I'd seen before. Initially, I thought they were Mom's from when she was young, but then I noticed that the handwritten dates predated her 1923 birth year.

Then I finally saw a name I recognized: Ruby. Of course. "These boxes belonged to Grandma Ruby," I announced to Mom, though she didn't seem interested in looking at their contents herself.

Overjoyed at finding a family time capsule, I immediately started to carefully unpack them. The photos were dated from 1910 to 1922, and they were well-maintained because of the dry Nevada climate and the cool darkness of my mom's closet. The loose pages must have been from Grandma Ruby's photo albums, but there were no binders to keep the pages together. Almost like she—or someone—had intended to throw them away, but just couldn't bring themselves to do it.

I was thumbing through the pages when I noticed a handwritten caption under a picture which said 'Our Wedding,' dated June 8, 1915. I was excited when I realized it was of Grandma Ruby, wearing a wedding dress and holding a bouquet of flowers. Since I had never met or seen my grandfather before, I was curious to see what he looked like.

I showed the photos to my mom, and she confirmed it was her mother, but then quickly looked away. It was almost like she couldn't bring herself to look at the pictures for too long for fear of getting scolded. For some reason I had a feeling she knew more than she was willing to tell me. And yes, I believe she may have played the 'dementia card.' She knew I would never pressure her for information that she couldn't remember.

The crazy thing about dementia is you just never know what the mind can remember or which memories have been stolen. Besides, Mom had always been an extremely strong-willed and tight-lipped woman, even before the signs of dementia appeared. If she did know more about the photos, clearly there would be no way of getting the information I needed from her. So I kept on going through the old photos, hoping more details would be revealed to me.

I found a newspaper clipping dated August 10, 1921 at the bottom of one of the boxes. It was the formal wedding announcement for my grandparents, which included a wedding photo of the new bride and groom. Except the groom standing next to my grandma was not the same man in the other photos, dated 1915. When I realized the dates on the wedding photos were different, I asked my mom if Grandma had been married before she married Grandpa. She shook her head adamantly, and continued to watch her TV game show.

I questioned my mom several more times about whether the bride in both photos was Grandma Ruby, and was met with the same results. I was amused by the thought that my grandma might have been secretly married to a gentleman prior to my grandfather, and I was determined to find out who this mystery man was. I grabbed Mom's old magnifying glass from the coffee table—the one she used years ago when she did her daily word puzzles, but which was now covered in dust.

The newspaper announcement from 1921 made it easy for me to identify the groom, because it gave the names of everyone who'd attended the wedding that day. However, identifying the people in the 1915 wedding photos was considerably more difficult. I could tell it was Grandma Ruby wearing the wedding dress and veil, but the caption underneath only said 'Our Wedding.' There were no names to identify the groom or the other two people in the picture.

The gentleman standing to the left of my grandma was wearing a dark suit and tie with a boutonniere on his left collar. There was also another man, and a woman in formal dress. The men were wearing bowler hats. All were standing underneath a large shade tree. Clearly it was a traditional wedding photograph, but with such little information I was still confused. However, I'm good at solving complex problems at work, and I was determined to solve this mystery.

I found numerous pictures of the same people dated from 1915 to 1920. I kept staring at the two men, thinking that something didn't look right. I was examining one of the photos when I noticed that both of the men had unusually small features, and their suits were ill-fitting: the jackets were falling off their shoulders, and the sleeves and pant legs had been rolled underneath because they were too long. Both of the gentlemen were wearing bowler hats, and it looked like their hair was tucked underneath. I thought to myself that men back then wouldn't have had long hair.

It took me a few more minutes to wrap my brain around what I was seeing. Then all of a sudden it hit me: it wasn't a man standing next to my grandmother in the wedding photos! I felt the blood rush to my head, and the back of my neck started to tingle as I fell back into my chair in disbelief. At the same time, I felt an incredible warmth flow over me. It was like being wrapped in a warm blanket after being stuck out in the cold for too long. It was an incredible feeling, and one that I will never forget. To this day I become overwhelmed with emotion thinking about that realization.

I firmly believe Grandma Ruby was with me at that moment, giving me a big hug, thankful that the truth had finally been revealed.

I spent the rest of that evening and into the next day just staring at those photos and crying. I wasn't sure why I was so emotional about them until I was driving back home to Los Angeles the next day. During the four-hour drive, I cried again, and then I realized that I didn't feel so different or alone anymore. It was the first time in my life that I didn't feel like the family oddball because of who I loved. I was no longer the only one.

THREE

As soon as I got home, I started unpacking the photos, letters, and newspaper articles and putting them in chronological order. There were letters and cards dating back as far as 1910. I was obsessed with the photos, and spent every day of the next couple of years searching the internet looking for clues to find out who the women in them were.

During that time I showed some of the photos to Aunt Patty, hoping her eighty-seven-year-old memory would be slightly better than my eighty-nine-year-old mother's. As I handed her one of the photos, I told her about the boxes I'd found, and asked if she knew any of the people in the picture. My aunt smiled, and began tracing an invisible circle with her thumb around Grandma Ruby's face.

I patiently waited for her to collect her memories and share any information that might be helpful. After a couple of minutes she broke the silence. "I know that's my mother, but I don't know who those other people are."

I thought that might be the end of our visit, until she said, "Our mother never talked about when she was a young girl, but she sure did love those old photos."

She had my full attention. "What do you mean?" I asked.

As Aunt Patty gazed at her mother's picture, I could tell she was reliving her past. "Me and your mother grew up with those boxes. Our mother insisted on dragging those damn things with us everywhere we moved. She never did anything with them except put them in her closet or under the bed, but she made sure they were on the moving truck if it was the last thing she did. In fact, your mom and me often accused her of loving those boxes more than she did us kids. I'm actually surprised your mother agreed to keep them after what happened."

"What happened, Aunt Patty?" I asked softly, so as not to break her train of thought.

"When we were teenagers your mother got it in her head she was going to find out what was so important in those boxes. When she finally mustered the courage to look inside, she found only old photos and newspaper articles that our mother had collected from when she was young in Wisconsin. Your mom asked who the people were, and your grandmother was furious. I still remember that day, because I had never seen either of them so upset before."

The room was silent as I watched her place the photo of her mother on the coffee table in front of us. Then she rubbed her hand across her forehead and eyes. She had grown tired, and I could tell her memory had faded.

It finally occurred to me that the boxes I had found in my mother's closet were the same two stacked in the corner of my aunt's living room in 1972—the ones delivered to our home in Los Angeles two weeks after Grandma's funeral.

I remembered the day they arrived. Mom still didn't know what to do with them. She'd stared at them where they sat in the living room. The fate of my grandmother's old photos and letters was in my mother's hands, and in the end she decided to do what her mother had always done with them—she put them in her closet.

For some reason Mom had no desire to open the boxes, but neither was she willing to discard them. Maybe out of respect for her mother, or maybe just because her mother had spent so many years safeguarding them. That was where the boxes had stayed until she and Dad retired and moved to Pahrump, Nevada in 1982. Then they were safely moved again from one closet to another, where they remained unopened until 2010, patiently waiting for me to discover them.

FOUR

I began researching the pictures, matching the people and events in the photos with those chronicled in the archived local newspapers, familiar names and places started to emerge. I concluded that there were not just one or two different women involved, but rather a larger group of women who had found a way to connect with each other in the middle of farm country. But I kept asking myself, "How and why Amherst, Wisconsin?"

I started to imagine how difficult it must have been for anyone back then to love someone of the same sex, and couldn't help comparing my grandma's life to my own. When I came out in the late 80s, it was difficult to know who to trust because of the stigma associated with being gay, even though coming out in a city like Los Angeles was far less dangerous than in other parts of the country.

Growing up, I didn't know anyone who was openly gay or lesbian, although the two women who lived across the street were rumored to be more than just friends. People would refer to them as "those lesbos" or "dykes." I'd laugh at the snide comments, but inside I wanted to run and hide from the world. By that time I had already had my share of schoolgirl crushes on female teachers, and I knew I was one too.

Already painfully shy, I became even more withdrawn for fear that some of the negative slurs my friends used would be directed toward me.

Keeping people at arm's length was my way of safeguarding my secret from the world.

Then it happened. When I was nineteen years old, I played guitar in a band in college, and I fell in love with the lead singer, Norma. It was like nothing I had ever felt before. I knew then that that was what falling in love should feel like. Mind you, falling in love with Norma did not change who I was: it simply reaffirmed my sexual orientation. However, as beautiful, natural, and wonderful as it was… I was petrified.

The fear became very real when I found myself looking over the Palos Verdes cliffs and watching the waves crash below. I don't remember driving there, but I do recall thinking how easy it would be to take those two steps forward and end my fear forever. It was at that point that it occurred to me I did *not* have a choice about who I loved, but I did have a choice about which direction those next two steps would take me in. I took two steps backward, turned around and retrieved the camera from my car. After taking a couple of pictures, I left the cliffs and never returned.

I tried to explain that to my mom when I broke the news about being a lesbian, but she was too upset to hear it. She asked me several times, "How could this have happened?" I didn't have an answer for her then, and I still wouldn't. There was never an outside influence in my life, one way or the other, that *caused* me to be a lesbian. There was no magical date or event in my life calendar that I could point to and say, "Yep, that's when I became a lesbian." It is simply a part of who I am.

Of course my inquisitive, well-meaning heterosexual friends would inevitably ask 'that' question: "When did you know you were gay?"

I would shrug and pretend to search for the magical date and time to give them, but honestly I've always known. I tried putting things in perspective by asking them, "When did you know you were straight?"

After I watched them struggle with that equally irrelevant question for a while, I could almost see the light bulb go on over their head. That's when I knew they understood. We are all simply who we are, and love is not a matter of choice.

I've always been extremely grateful for being loved and accepted by my family and friends. Some of my LGBTQ (lesbian, gay, bisexual, transgender, queer/questioning) friends were not so lucky. It was common to hear about people who were kicked out of their homes by parents who refused to accept them for who they loved. Some, but not all, fell into the darkness of depression, drug abuse, or alcoholism.

Although society has become more accepting, sadly the percentage of homeless and runaway youth who identify as LGBTQ remains extremely high in America.

However, even with all the love and support of my family and friends, I always felt like the 'square peg.' I think that's why finding my grandma's photos had such a profound effect on me. Because regardless of how loved and supported someone feels, when you are young, being different is very difficult, especially when it comes to one's sexuality.

I still have the photos I took when I was nineteen, overlooking the Palos Verde cliffs. Sometimes I look at them to remind myself how beautiful life is.

FIVE

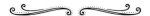

2014

For the next several years, I spent hundreds of hours researching archived newspaper articles on the internet, and I became a member of the Wisconsin Historical Society. I was looking for answers to questions about places and people I knew nothing about. But even with all of the online research I did, something was missing. I had a deep need to see, in person, the house where my grandmother lived, and to walk the streets she had walked. I needed to see the lakes she swam in, the trees and rocks she climbed, and to visit the places where so many of the photos had been taken. Most importantly, I needed to breathe the air and smell the ground where everything had happened. Yes—I needed to go to Amherst, Wisconsin.

I assumed things had likely changed considerably in the little town of Amherst over the last one hundred years, but I wanted to see it for myself. I prepared myself for a town that was either overdeveloped or rundown. It seems like time has a way of changing places, especially small farming towns like Amherst, often for the worse.

I planned a business trip to Chicago in the middle of March 2014. After my last meeting, I packed up my rental car and set my GPS for Amherst. I was looking forward to the four-hour drive and to seeing the wide-open Wisconsin landscape.

Three hours into the drive, I started recognizing the names of towns and cities my grandmother had mentioned in her cards and letters: Oshkosh, Appleton, New London, Waupaca. At every town I recognized, I laughed and cheered out loud. It was like I was living a dream that was slowly turning into a reality. It also cracked me up that a West Coast city girl would know so much about a place I had never been. I'm sure some people driving next to me thought I was crazy, but I didn't care. I was coming home for the first time in a hundred years.

I loved every mile and every minute of the long drive. The landscape was beautiful, with old country barns and wide-open land—things I wasn't used to, growing up in Los Angeles. I saw the train tracks that ran parallel to the highway, and couldn't help wondering if Grandma Ruby had taken those same tracks when she traveled to Milwaukee or Chicago to visit family and friends.

My GPS informed me, "Only two more miles to Amherst exit." Then the electronic voice announced it was only one mile. My heart was pounding so hard I thought it might burst out of my chest; my palms were sweating, and my breath was short from excitement. *Oh my God, I'm here!*

After taking the exit, I immediately pulled over to the side of the road. I sat there for a couple of minutes, trying to calm down. I wanted to take my time and breathe it all in. There would only be one first time to see everything, and I didn't want to miss or forget a moment of it. When I resumed driving, I was mesmerized by the old farmhouses and dairies leading me into town. My GPS said, "You have reached your destination." I laughed again at such an appropriate electronic message. But it was true... I *had* reached my destination.

The rush of cold Wisconsin wind that hit my face when I opened the car door was a chilling reminder that I was definitely not in Southern California anymore. As I stood to stretch my muscles, I took in my first full breath of Amherst air. I could smell rich soil, damp from the early morning rain, and I noticed there was still a little snow along the north side of the Amherst Inn B&B.

The beautiful mauve-colored, Victorian-style house on Main Street stood like a proud monarch from the past. The owners, Bob and Tom, had told me ahead of time that they would both be attending a town meeting and wouldn't be able to greet me when I arrived. They left instructions for me on the unlocked front door on how to find my room.

When I walked into the Amherst Inn, I realized I was the only person in the house. The living room was silent; only the ticking sound of multiple clocks on the walls and mantel could be heard. Standing in the middle of this large home was oddly comforting, but it seemed like a dream. I started to examine the ornate glass doors, the tapestry-draped windows, and the hand-engraved woodwork leading to the second floor. It gave me the surreal feeling of stepping back in time, and although the house was empty, I didn't feel alone.

I was energized and exhausted at the same time while I toted my bags from the car to my room. I sat down to rest for a moment in one of the vintage chairs in the front room, taking in a deep breath of the old home. I could smell the sweet smokiness of the old wood and feel the history in the walls.

Based on the age and location of the house, it was highly likely that at some point my grandmother had walked through the same front door I just had. My thoughts and imagination started racing. Did she hear the same creaking of the wooden floors as she walked down the hallway? Did she look at herself in the large decorative mirror that was built into the entrance of the house? It had been almost a hundred years since she left this little town, but time was standing still, and I sensed she was there to greet me.

Since I had many things I wanted to see and do on my visit, I quickly unpacked my cameras and computer. The downtown area was only two blocks from where I was staying, and I made my way there on foot. I was pleasantly surprised to find a little town that was neither rundown, nor overdeveloped. In fact, it was a wonderful place with many of the old store-fronts still in use; it looked very much like some of my grandma's photos.

The streets were quiet, with only an occasional car going by. I stood in the middle of Main Street to take a few pictures without fear of being hit—something I would never dare to do in Los Angeles. As I continued on my way, I couldn't help wondering what it would have been like to grow up in such a small town a hundred years ago. Walking the same path my grandmother had, my mind flipped between the present day and 1914.

It was so easy to envision my grandmother walking down these same streets. There was the general store where she would have shopped for flour and other home goods, and the post office where she picked up her mail. I also found the old phone company she'd worked at in 1917, and noticed a set of stairs she would have climbed to report to work as the town phone girl. The town did have some more modern buildings, but for the most part seemed as if it had managed to resist the urge to overdevelop. Yes, in many ways it was the same small town where my grandmother had taken photographs, laughed, prayed, cried and loved.

By the time I got back to the B&B, the owners were home. A wonderful couple, Bob and Tom had been together over twenty years. Coincidentally, Bob was the president of the local historical society, so I was hoping he would be able to identify some of the locations where the photos had been taken. They were both amazed to see all the pictures I had of the old town. Then I showed them my grandmother's wedding photos. Neither one of them could believe what they were looking at. Since same-sex marriage was not yet legal in Wisconsin, the impact of the images was obvious. I watched tears swell in their eyes.

As they looked through the photos, they told me where some of them were taken. Bob informed that the town library had a lot of old newspapers and photos that I might find interesting.

The next morning I walked through town again to the local library. It was a small building, but seemed modern enough, with computers sitting at some of the front tables. I figured that was a good sign. When I checked in with the head librarian at the front desk, she pointed me in the direction of their town historical room. I expected to see a research area where I could review old microfilm to find more information about my family. However, the space was barely larger than a closet, filled floor-to-ceiling with stacks of old newspapers and binders. The librarian seemed a little embarrassed about the disarray; she explained that none of the documents had been digitized yet, but someday they would be. I thought to myself, *This would explain why I couldn't find some of the information I was looking for online.* She showed me how to look up people by using the little wooden card-catalog box. It was truly a vision from the pre-computer days.

Once I got the hang of the card-catalog system, I started looking up the names of all the people I knew, and found my great-grandmother, Hilda W. Peterson. The card gave me the stack number, date, and page to find her information. I located the correct stack of newspapers, then flipped through them until I saw her obituary in the *Amherst Gazette* from August 3, 1912. It didn't explain how she died: it only said that she was taken with a sudden fainting spell and had failed to regain consciousness. I'm guessing it was probably a heart attack or stroke that took her life. What I found so interesting was how the newspaper article described her. It talked about how "well-known and respected" she was, and how she was "one of the most progressive and influential" residents in the area.

I didn't know a lot about history at the time, but I did know those were not standard terms used to describe most women during this era. Generally, women during this period of time were referred to as 'good' or 'loving' wives and mothers to those who survived them, and certainly words like 'respected,' 'progressive,' or 'influential,' were not used to describe commonplace housewives. The description of my great-grandmother in that obituary gave me great insight to her strong and independent character. I could only imagine how difficult it would have been for my Grandma

Ruby, and her siblings Leroy and Ada, when their mother passed; they were the only remaining children still living at home.

When I went to the library, I was initially only planning to spend a couple of hours there, but I ended up spending half the day. I looked through original newspapers from the early 1900s. The pages were yellow and brittle with age, and had a musty smell to them. I was hesitant to touch them for fear they would fall apart. However, holding the original newspapers in my hands made me feel connected to my family in a way I was not expecting. I could almost envision Grandma Ruby, her parents, and their neighbors reading the same newspaper to catch up on local social events or the price of a new cow. I became lost in the fantasy of what it would have been like to live in this little town one hundred years ago. Suddenly the librarian cleared her throat—a subtle reminder that it was getting late, and the library would be closing soon.

I gathered up all my notes, and took pictures of other newspaper articles with my phone. I was happy to have found information about my great-grandmother, Hilda, and was most pleased to discover the exact location of the Peterson family farmhouse on old county land maps. Up until that point I'd only known that their home was next to Lime Lake, but the property maps showed me exactly where to go.

Before starting my journey to write this book, I knew nothing about my grandmother's younger years growing up on the farm in Amherst. And the only thing I knew about her parents—my great-grandparents—was that they were immigrants from Sweden. Beyond that, I had no idea who these people were. Intrigued by the large missing part of my genealogy, I started doing research online about my long-lost Peterson family members.

After reading a multitude of archived newspaper articles and viewing old family photos, a timeline of events started to emerge. Not only did I find out what they were doing one hundred years ago, I also started to understand who they were.

This is my account of the Peterson family from 1912-1920, which is based on the facts I uncovered, as well as my own creative interpretation of events.

SIX

Ruby was sixteen when her mother passed away from an unexplained and sudden illness on April 12,1912. Since her older brothers and sisters had already moved out of the house, that left Ruby and her eleven-year-old brother Leroy to take care of their grieving father, Peter Peterson, and the family farm. Her older sister, Ada, was eighteen, and had just left home the year before to finish studying to become a teacher.

There was only so much Ruby and Leroy could do. Between the household chores and the work to be done around the farm, things quickly fell into a state of disorder. It was a matter of time before Peter Peterson sent for Ada to help him manage the farm and her two younger siblings. She begrudgingly agreed to come home, but only after she received her teaching certificate in the fall.

In the meantime, because Ruby was the only female on the farm, she was expected to prepare all the meals, clean the house, do the laundry, milk the cows, keep the bookkeeping current, and help Leroy with his homework. There was no time for her to grieve the loss of her mother, not even at bedtime. As soon as Ruby started to feel her eyes prickle with tears as she thought about her mother, exhaustion would kick in, and sleep quickly took over.

Ruby knew Ada hated coming back home after working so hard to earn her teaching certificate, but she was overjoyed. The farmhands were happy about Ada's return as well, because they didn't care much for Ruby's cooking. Sometimes the smell of burnt biscuits would waft over all five acres of land. The workers cringed at the smell, but knew better than to give her grief over it. Although she was only five-foot-three, Ruby could throw a bale of hay just as far as they could. Plus, her sharp wit could easily cut any man down to size.

Not being a girly-girl, Ruby figured out early on that she wasn't like the other young ladies in town. With her unusually assertive behavior, most people considered her too aggressive and sometimes difficult to deal with, but in a charming kind of way. In a time when women were striving for their right to vote, in her mind she already had the same rights as men—and she acted like it.

Generally the only two people able to manage Ruby's wild behavior were her mother and her sister, Ada. Although Ada was considerably less impulsive than her younger sister, she too yearned for independence: that was why she aspired to become a teacher.

Ruby had briefly attended a school that prepared high school students for teaching jobs. Her parents hoped she would follow in her sister's footsteps. However, Ruby quite often found herself getting into trouble with instructors, usually because she was talking too much, or making the other girls laugh in the back of the classroom. This was the case for all of her classes except one.

English had quickly become Ruby's favorite class; however, that had little to do with the subject matter. For this class, Ruby made sure to be on her best behavior. She sat quietly in the first row, and aligned her desk perfectly in front of her instructor's seat. Waiting for class to begin, she held her breath, knowing her favorite teacher would soon enter the room.

It's normal for all young eyes to look up when their teacher enters the classroom. But when Miss Emily Phillips entered, all eyes were drawn to her studious and striking good looks. Her presence commanded attention from people regardless of age.

Her dark brown hair was pulled back tight into a schoolmarm bun, and her posture was perfect. Ruby watched Miss Phillips as she gathered books from her desk to begin the lesson of the day. Once her silver wire-rimmed reading glasses were resting firmly on the bridge of her nose, she delivered her instructions to the class. Ruby's eyes followed in a daze as her teacher walked around the room reading from the textbook. She was mesmerized by Miss Phillips in her layered, ivory-colored dress, which seemed to float as she moved from student to student.

Such attention from her young pupil did not go unnoticed by Miss Phillips. Occasionally, Ruby's stare was broken when her teacher tilted her head forward to peer over her reading glasses. "Ruby, did you need help with something?"

Ruby blushed as she emerged from her daydream. "No ma'am, Miss Phillips. I'm done." With her pencil down, she waited for another opportunity to gaze at her favorite instructor.

Unfortunately, this was the only class Ruby successfully completed. Eventually she was forced to drop out of school, after her math instructor suggested to her parents that she would be better suited for marriage than a teaching profession. Ruby was concerned at first because she knew her father wanted her to be a teacher like her sister. She knew the instructor was right about her not becoming a teacher, but she hated the notion of marriage. Ruby's disappointment at leaving school was compounded by the fact that she would no longer be able to enjoy the company of Miss Phillips.

A few weeks after she left school, Ruby could hardly believe her eyes when she pulled a photo postcard from the mailbox. The front of the card had a portrait of her favorite teacher, with her hair pulled back and her glasses pushed up to her eyes. Ruby's heart pounded as she ran her finger over the most beautiful picture she had ever seen.

A note on the back of the card read:

Dear Ruby,

Although you are not my pupil now, I don't want you to

think I have forgotten about you. Please remember I am still your friend.
Emily Phillips

I found this photo postcard along with Grandma Ruby's other well-protected letters and photos.

After her education ended, along with any possibility of becoming a teacher, Ruby was free to pursue things she was much more interested in, like climbing trees or fishing with the local farm boys. Much to the dismay of her father, Ruby continued these activities throughout her teenage years.

Ruby's father was concerned that she seemed more interested in playing with the boys than dating them. Even after the death of his beloved wife, Peter would often look to the sky and ask for her guidance. "What are we going to do about that girl, Hilda?"

Although there was no physical answer from his wife, he could imagine her sweet Swedish voice telling him, "Don't worry so much, Peter, she'll grow out of it. I did the same things when I was young and I turned out just fine."

Peter's usual rebuttal was, "Yes, but she'll be twenty years old in a couple of years. What man is going to want to marry a woman who likes to climb trees?"

The only answer he received was the silence and loneliness he felt as a father trying to raise a young teenage girl without her mother.

The line of young men interested in Ruby was not short. Her striking blue eyes and smile melted the hearts of many suitable callers in the area. They often asked her to dances in town, but were quickly disappointed when she told them she already had plans. She loved to dance, but preferred not going to such events with an arranged partner. She would rather go with her friends: that way she could dance with whomever she wanted to.

Growing up, Ruby never liked feeling that she didn't have options or that she belonged to someone. Unlike most young ladies, she never gave much thought to finding a boyfriend, and never understood why someone would settle for a man who would want to take away her freedom. That just didn't make any sense to her.

Ruby dreamed of leaving the farm and the little town of Amherst someday, to travel the country and see the world. Even though they lived five miles from the station, she could hear the rumble of the huge steam-engine train as it pulled into town. The best part of her day was hearing the 9:00 p.m. train whistle blow just before it entered the station. Even in the dead of winter, she would leave her bedroom window open just enough to hear the gentle sound of the train as the freezing Wisconsin air pushed though her tapestry drapes. Bundled up in blankets, she waited for it. Only once she'd heard it did she allow her eyes to grow heavy, and dream.

SEVEN

August 1913

In 1913, Ruby's father brought home a Seneca No. 3 Trio Folding Camera. It wasn't a new camera; he had received it in trade from one of the local farmers for work he had done. He figured Leroy and his two sisters would enjoy it, and that it might take their minds off missing their mother. He even hoped it would inspire the three of them to use their idle time more productively, since they seemed to find endless ways of getting into mischief.

It didn't take much time before Leroy started taking photos around the farm and of his sisters. With Ruby and Ada directing him, he became the official family photographer. Of course, Leroy was already accustomed to receiving direction from his two older sisters. But he rather enjoyed the time spent setting up the camera and adjusting the speed of the lens based on the changing light of day.

Ruby called out, "Come on, Leroy, we don't have all day. Take the picture, will ya?"

She was frustrated, and she could tell Leroy was too when he yelled back, "Hold your darn horses sister, I'm almost done! I need to make sure your face is in focus, that's all."

Ruby had been sitting on top of the hay bale for almost twenty minutes in the hot August sun before she climbed down to find out what was taking Leroy so long. To calm his sister down, he quickly explained how the camera worked, and then showed her what he was trying to do with the different lens settings and shutter speeds. By the time she returned to the top of the hay bale, she had a good understanding of how to operate the seemingly complicated device.

That evening after supper, Ruby took the camera to Lime Lake, which was located just down the road from the house. The setting sun was just below the tree line, and the azure sky was already beginning to darken. Ruby walked quickly to ensure she would have time to adjust the shutter speed to its slowest setting before the sun set completely.

She often walked to the lake after her household chores were done; however, that night was different. The full August moon was hanging high in the sky, and she wanted to capture the moonbeams that would surely be dancing on the lake.

The warm summer breeze pushed past her as she made her way to the lake. The twilight song of robins could be heard all around her as darkness slowly engulfed the forest. Soon the rhythmic chirping of crickets would become louder, along with the deep, resonating serenade of bull-frogs. Once the camera was set up, Ruby sat in darkness listening to the symphony of sounds that completed the day.

This would be the first of many photos Ruby would take to remind her of the beautiful things in her life. After she took it, she sat there for a few more minutes thinking about what she wanted to do in life. She knew she had to make a plan soon, because at the ripe old age of seventeen she was already feeling the pressure from her family to find a fellow, get married, and start having children. The whispered talk from some townspeople about her lack of a steady beau was not helping.

Options were very limited for young women. If she wasn't going to school, or didn't have a respectable job as a teacher or nurse, she was expected to find a man and be a good wife and mother.

Ruby prayed that someday she would find a man who would change her mind about settling down. But that dream seemed so far away, and she didn't understand why. As hard as she tried, she never envisioned herself walking down the aisle wearing a wedding dress like her sisters.

She rationalized her disinterest by telling herself, *I just haven't met the right fellow yet, that's all.* She would daydream that she'd find her perfect husband as he was getting off the train from Chicago. Their eyes would meet, and they would fall deeply and passionately in love. After they got married, they would move to Chicago, and she would dine at all the most popular restaurants and shop at all the finest boutiques for new dresses. They would live in a big, beautiful house and have four children—two boys and two girls—and they would all live happily ever after. Every time Ruby completed the story in her mind, she prayed to God she would start believing in it someday.

She was brought back to reality by the sound of breaking leaves and twigs from someone walking in the woods behind her. It was Leroy and his dog, Foxy; since she had the camera with her, she was sure he was looking for it.

"There you are. I've been looking everywhere for you," Leroy said as he cleared a path toward his sister.

"Was it me or the camera you were looking for?" Ruby asked sarcastically.

Leroy sat next to her. "Well, I reckon both. Pa's been looking for you for an hour because he needs you to fix a tear on his jacket pocket before he leaves on his business trip tomorrow. And I wanted to clean the camera so I can take a few pictures of him before he goes."

Ruby kept looking out at the moonbeams sparkling off of the lake. Without blinking, she asked her brother, "Are you going to get married someday, Leroy?"

He was perplexed by her question, and stared blankly at her for a moment. "Of course I am, someday. Why?"

She didn't respond to his question, instead asking another: "What do you think she'll look like?"

Without any hesitation, Leroy responded, "She'll have long, wavy light-brown hair, beautiful blue eyes, and hopefully she'll know how to cook just as good as Ma did."

Ruby couldn't help noticing how easy and spontaneous Leroy's response was. He had no doubt what was going to happen in his life. She kept looking out at the lake and asked another question. "Are you going to have children?"

Leroy was starting to get annoyed by his sister's strange interrogation, and answered abruptly, "I'm sure I will. Isn't that what's supposed to happen?"

Without a word, Ruby handed Leroy the camera, got up and started walking quickly back toward the house.

Leroy remained seated. "Hey, where are you going and why are you acting so strange, sis?"

She shouted back, "I'm going home to fix Pa's jacket pocket. Isn't that what's supposed to happen?"

That was all Ruby could say without Leroy knowing how upset she was; her throat was tight with emotions. Once she was safely out of view of her brother she allowed her tears to fall. On her walk back to the home, she asked herself, "*How is it possible that my younger brother knows what he should do? Why do I feel so lost? What's wrong with me? Why am I so different?*

Ruby asked herself these same questions often. Every Sunday morning at church, sitting next to her family and friends, she secretly prayed for God to make her thoughts 'normal.' To make her think, feel, and desire the same things that everyone else did. *Life would be so much easier,* she thought.

EIGHT

April 1914

Ruby, now eighteen; Ada, twenty; and Leroy, thirteen, had free rein of the house and the farm. Ada was focused on getting one of the few open teaching positions available in Amherst. She also had her hands full looking after her younger siblings and helping with the bookkeeping for the farm when their father was out of town, which was often. Ada noticed Ruby wasn't in a hurry to find a husband, nor was she eager to take on added responsibilities around the farm.

There were plenty of chores to be done around the farm, and their father made sure Leroy and Ruby's young hands were kept busy. As a reward for hard work he took them on camping trips to some of the local lakes. With Ruby and her bother getting older, he hoped someday soon they'd be leaving home to get married and have children; although he wasn't sure if that day would ever come for Ruby.

In the meantime, he had a business to run and would leave them on their own for days or sometimes weeks at a time. The five older kids were already married and had moved on to start their own families. Occasionally, one of them would stop by to check on their younger siblings, but most of the time the three of them only had each other to depend on.

There were still remnants of snow at the edges of some of the trees and houses, but the Midwest landscape was starting to give way to spring.

The breeze was brisk as winter fought to hold on, but the skeleton trees refused the notion and were beginning to show signs of life, a reward for enduring months of snow and freezing temperatures of another blustery Wisconsin winter. The change of seasons meant growth, and the hope of warmer weather around the corner. Soon the ground would be soft enough for potato-planting season to start. This meant months of hard work tending to the fields and livestock in the heat of the summer, until the fall harvest. But for now, the euphoria of being outside and feeling the warm sun was all that mattered.

The three of them often raced each other to see who could complete their daily farm chores first. The loser would usually get stuck with doing the dishes. By this time, Leroy was fastest at doing his chores; he rarely needed to worry about doing dishes. Little did Leroy know that Ruby and Ada really didn't mind doing the dishes, and used the challenge as a way to get him to hurry up so they would have more time to get cleaned up and go into town after the work was done.

Leroy usually didn't care much about going into town with his sisters. He would rather spend his days at Lime Lake, fishing or skipping rocks across the water. Nevertheless, that day he was eager to go into town, because Ada had promised to buy him candy as a reward for getting an 'A' on his last math test.

As soon as the dishes were cleaned and put away, the girls ran up the stairs to get ready for their trip into town. Ruby was looking for her favorite dress. Most of them were handed down from her three older sisters, and a couple had belonged to her mother. She would often re-sew them to look new and stylish. Since Ada had continued her education and attended school in Stevens Point, her dresses were always more expensive and fashionable. They both chose to wear their favorite dresses, but not their best dresses. Those they would save for special occasions.

Ruby had on her light-yellow dress, and found a long strand of her mother's white ribbon in the sewing room. She looked down at the ribbon in her hands before slowly tying it around her hair, thinking about how much she missed her mother. She opened one of her mother's bottles of rose perfume and closed her eyes as she breathed in her mother's scent. After placing a few drops behind each ear and on her wrists, she was ready to go into town.

Leroy was waiting for the girls outside, passing time by throwing rocks into the open field in front of their house. "Finally, you two ready? What takes girls so long to get ready anyways? We're only going into town for a couple of hours, and you know everyone there. Who are you two trying to impress?"

The girls knew he was right; they did know everyone in town. Ruby responded quickly, "Well, for your information, ladies always need to look their best. We never know who may roll into town on the train, whisk us off our feet, and take us away on a trip around the world."

Leroy just shook his head, knowing there was no arguing with his sisters. "Oh, brother. Let's get goin' then."

The three of them started the long walk toward town. It was only a ten-minute walk along the gravel farmhouse road to the hard dirt highway, but it would take another hour to reach town by foot. If they were lucky, someone they knew would drive by so they could hitch a ride. Since everyone in that area knew each other, they had a good chance of that happening.

They reached the main highway and started heading toward Amherst. Soon the three of them could hear the sound of a car approaching from behind, and turned around to see a cloud of dust heading their way. They couldn't make out who it was yet, but whoever it was, they were driving very fast. Suddenly Ada recognized the driver, from her long blonde curls flailing in the wind. She screamed out her name and started waving her arms over her head. "Cora, stop! Stop!" Cora came to a stop as a cloud of dust billowed past them and the new convertible Model-T she was driving.

"What are you pretty girls up to? Oh…and boy," Cora said.

Leroy was irritated at Cora's remark and rolled his eyes back at her. But he was happy for a ride into town, so he decided not to respond.

Cora lived down the road from the Peterson farm, and was well-known around town—mostly because of the parties and social events held at her home. She was famous for motoring down roads as fast as her convertible Model T would take her, preferably with the top down. She was also one of the few women in the area without a husband, and who owned her own property, including two cars.

Ruby waved the cloud of dust away from her face. After the air cleared, she said, "We're heading into town to see what kind of trouble we can get into."

Cora's smile widened. "That's my kind of thinking." Cora always fancied the Peterson girls, and thought there was something a little wild about the two Swedish sisters, especially Ruby. "Hop in and let's go for a ride into the big town of Amherst."

Ada climbed into the front seat, and Ruby and Leroy sat in the back. For Leroy, the ride seemed to take forever, even though it was only a few minutes. He was in the back seat, just watching the road going by; all he could hear was the girls gossiping about people in town and cackling like hens. As soon as he saw the railroad bridge that crossed over Main Street, he knew the painful ordeal was almost over with.

He hardly waited for the car to stop before jumping onto Main Street. The three girls looked at each other and started laughing. "I don't know what you girls think is so funny," Leroy said, as he started walking to the corner candy store.

Cora noticed his annoyance and called out, "Isn't that just like a boy, to head for the first candy store he sees."

The three of them laughed even harder. When they'd caught their breath, Cora asked, "Say, do you gals like to play cards?"

Ruby and Ada both responded "Yes," in unison.

"Well, good!" Cora said. "I'm having a few of my lady friends over this Saturday afternoon to play some cards, and I'll have music and refreshments between games. It would be grand if you two could join us. It's surely going to be a very lively party."

Knowing that their father would be out of town until the middle of the next week, Ada and Ruby didn't hesitate in their decision to attend Cora's party.

"Fabulous. I'll see you both before two o'clock on Saturday, then. And don't be late, you'll not want to miss a minute of this party." Cora slammed the Model-T into gear and stepped on the gas pedal as hard as she could. A cloud of dark exhaust came pouring out from the back of the car as she turned left onto Lincoln Street, heading to the north end of town.

The girls were thrilled to be invited, because some of Cora's parties were very exclusive. It seemed there was always someone exciting coming in from Chicago or Milwaukee just to go to her house for a social event.

The sisters started walking toward the center of town, which was only two blocks away. Right before they entered the dress shop on the corner, Ruby said, "I wish I had a new dress to wear. All of mine look so drab."

Ada responded, "What do you mean? I love your dresses."

"I reckon you should; most of them were yours before I got them," Ruby responded.

Ada stopped walking. "Now, sister, I told you before not to say 'reckon.' That is not a word." The teacher and mentor side of Ada would often come out when her younger siblings used improper English. After the grammar correction, Ada walked into the shop. "Now let's go look at some of these dresses. I'm sure we can fix some of yours to look just as good as the ones in here."

Mrs. Wells was working behind the counter. She saw the Peterson girls walk into her shop, but didn't pay them much attention. She knew they had no money to purchase anything. Ruby pointed to the dress in the window. "Oh, look at that dress, Ada. It would be perfect for Cora's party."

At that point Mrs. Wells looked up from the counter and asked, "Does your daddy know what you two are up to? That Cora girl is trouble with a capital T."

"Well of course he does," Ada said firmly. "He knows perfectly well about the party, and told us we could go."

Ruby looked worried, so Ada whispered, "What's wrong?"

In a hushed voice Ruby asked, "Do you suppose we'll get in trouble if Daddy finds out about the party?"

"Stop your worrying, Ruby! Daddy doesn't care. Besides, he has nothing to worry about, because he won't find out...right?"

"I suppose." Ruby grimaced.

Although Ruby was the most adventurous in the family, she was also the most fearful of disappointing her father. She never wanted to fail him, although she knew she often did. Their father understood that Ada hadn't found a husband yet because she was working on becoming a teacher, but he couldn't figure out what to do with Ruby's aversion to courtship.

The girls stopped by the general store in the center of town to pick up a bag of flour, and then made their way through town, talking to all of the people and shop owners they knew on Main Street. They ended up back at the candy store, where Leroy was still hanging out front with some of his schoolmates. "We need to start heading home now, it's gonna be dark in another hour," he said.

They started walking home. However, this time they weren't so lucky; no one came by to give them a ride. They took all the shortcuts they knew, through pastures and along the riverside, finally arriving at their front door just after sunset.

It was dark enough that they didn't notice the buggy parked by the side of the house. When they opened the front door, Elmer, their older brother, was sitting and waiting for them in their mother's old chair. "So, what have you three been up to?" he asked.

All three of them were startled, and Ruby screamed. "Elmer, you nearly scared us to death. What in the world are you doing here?"

Elmer was four years older than Ada, and was going to college in Stevens Point to study accounting. "I decided I needed to check on you three and the farm, since Daddy's been out of town on business for a while, and I'm glad I did. Where have you three been? Why is there no supper on the stove?"

Ada and Leroy looked at each other; they had no idea what to say.

All of a sudden, Ruby said very calmly, "We needed to go into town and buy some flour." As she showed the bag of flour to Elmer, she proceeded to tell him, "We work just as hard as the men do on this farm, and we can take care of ourselves."

Elmer raised his eyebrows and tilted his head toward Ada and Leroy as if to question the two of them separately. "Flour?" he asked. They both nodded their heads adamantly. "Well, if you two say so... Ada, I will talk with you later."

Elmer leaned back in their mother's chair and said, "Go ahead and start cooking then, I'm starving. I've been traveling all day just to check on you three brats."

Since the passing of their mother, Elmer knew it was difficult for the three remaining kids. He also knew that their father, who had not been the disciplinarian, had little or no control over his younger brother and two sisters.

Ada and Ruby ran into the kitchen to start supper while Elmer and Leroy went into the sitting room to read the daily newspaper. Elmer took this opportunity to question Leroy about how things were going around the farm, and to make sure the girls weren't giving him too much of a hard time. Leroy knew to keep his mouth shut, and told Elmer what he wanted to hear. "Everything is going fine. It's just a little lonely around here being the only boy in the house, that's all."

While preparing dinner, Ruby asked Ada if she thought they were going to get into trouble.

Ada quickly turned around. "There you go again, worrying about getting into trouble. Don't you understand that as long as we can take care of ourselves, no one really wants to bother with us? Do you think that Dora and Charley or Perry and Bernice really want us living with them? No! I can tell you that none of them want that, and I sure don't want it either. That's why, as long as we don't hurt ourselves or someone else, we won't get into trouble. Now stop worrying so much, and make the biscuits before Elmer really has a fit. I just hope he doesn't stay here that long, because I want to go to Cora's party Saturday afternoon."

As it turned out, Elmer only stayed a couple of days. During that time, the three of them worked hard on the farm. Leroy did all of his homework and the girls got all the farm bookkeeping updated and made sure all of the household chores were done—though not with the same enthusiasm, since going into town wasn't an option.

Ada was visibly happy when she noticed Elmer was packing his bags on Saturday morning. "Oh, are you leaving so soon, brother?" she asked with a sly smile on her face.

Elmer wasn't facing her, but he could tell she was smiling as she asked the question. He slowly turned around and looked at her as he sat on the side of his bed. "Now Ada, you are the oldest one here, and you need to make sure those two don't get out of control. You need to set the example and be a mother figure for them. They need you. Can you do that for me?"

By that time Ada had a very serious look on her face, and said, "Of course, brother, you know I will. We'll be just fine. There's no need for you to worry so much about them, or me. Trust me."

Elmer wasn't sure he truly believed Ada, but he needed to head back to Stevens Point and do his homework before returning to school Monday morning.

Ruby and Ada watched Elmer pack up his belongings on the buggy. As soon as he started heading toward town, they knew they were free to get ready for Cora's party.

NINE

It took the girls most of that day to fix their hair and figure out what dresses to wear. Leroy had gone fishing even before his brother left, and had no idea what his sisters were up to. He headed back home from Lime Lake around noon. His dog, Foxy, bounded in front of him, paving the way home. Leroy was excited to show off to his sisters the string of trout he had caught at the lake. He walked into the house, but didn't see them anywhere. He flung the fish on the kitchen table and listened for them. He could hear the girls talking and laughing up in their room. As he walked upstairs, he could smell the rose perfume his sisters liked to wear when they were going to special events.

"Say, where are you two going all dressed up?" he asked.

Ruby proudly stated, "We are going to a card party this afternoon over at Cora Turner's house."

Leroy's eyes widened, and he asked, "Can I go to the party with you?"

Still looking at herself in the mirror, Ada told him, "It's a party for ladies only. And boys, especially fishy-smelling boys, are not allowed."

He just looked down and walked away, disappointed, as the sisters continued getting ready for the party. Neither of them were aware that their brother's feelings had been hurt.

It was almost one in the afternoon, and Ada was waiting for Ruby downstairs. "Ruby, hurry up, we don't want to be late!" she called out.

"I'm coming!" Ruby yelled back as she walked down the stairs.

Ada stood on the front porch, looking up into the cloudless blue sky. "Isn't it a wonderful day, Ruby?"

Ruby responded by looking up as well. "Yes, sister, it's a glorious day for a party." Both beamed at the fact that they were heading for Cora's house for the day.

The two sisters started off on the gravel road toward the main highway, feeling the warmth of the sun. Leroy watched his sisters leave without him and hollered out, "So you two ain't even gonna help me clean all these fish I brought home? Fine! That's just fine. Next time you two want some good fish for supper I'm just gonna hand you my fishin' pole and you can go catch them your own selves."

The girls could tell how upset their brother was, but kept on going like they hadn't heard a word he said. It was about a fifty-minute walk to Cora's, so they walked briskly, but not so fast as to get their best party dresses dirty. As they walked, the sisters started talking about who they might see at the party.

About five minutes into their walk on the main road, they heard a car sputtering down the road behind them. They didn't recognize the driver, and decided not to wave for a ride. The car passed them, but stopped suddenly. The convertible top was down, and the driver looked over his shoulder at them. "Say, you two ladies look like you're going to a party."

Ada and Ruby didn't recognize the gentleman, but he seemed friendly enough. The sisters glanced at each other briefly, and then Ada said, "Yes, we are going to a ladies' party over at Cora Turner's house this afternoon."

The gentleman smiled widely and said, "Great, me too! Do you want a lift?"

Ada and Ruby both looked perplexed, because they'd thought the party was just for ladies. Ruby stepped forward. "That would be lovely." Ada was still confused about why a gentleman would be going to a ladies' party, but followed Ruby to the car. Ada sat in the back and Ruby in the front as the driver slammed the Ford into gear and proceeded toward Cora's home.

Both the girls were unusually quiet for the first couple of minutes, until the driver looked over to the sisters and asked them their names. They both responded politely. Ruby noticed something odd about the gentleman, but before she could ask about it, he spoke. "People call me Fritz," he said. Ruby stared at Fritz, taking in his bowler hat and the driving gloves he was wearing. She also noticed that he was a small fellow and his suit didn't fit him very well. She thought he seemed quite pleasant, and attractive in a way she couldn't describe to herself.

Fritz sensed that Ruby was still staring, and asked her how long she had known Cora. "We've known Cora for ages. We are all the best of friends." Ruby stated.

There was another moment of awkward silence. "Have you girls been to one of Cora's card parties before?" Fritz asked.

Ada sat silently in the back seat, while Ruby did all of the talking. "We're always invited, but only attended a couple of times before." Ada knew that wasn't true, but didn't say a word.

Fritz, on the other hand, had attended many of Cora's parties in the past and didn't recall seeing either of the girls before. Surely if either of them had attended Cora's parties, he would have recalled seeing such pretty girls.

Fritz turned into the long driveway leading up to Cora's place. There were a few cars already parked around the house, and some people stood on the front porch talking. Fritz said, "It looks like some of my pals are here already."

He parked the car underneath a large shade tree at the side of the house. Before the sisters could exit the vehicle, Fritz jumped out and ran to the passenger side to open the door for them. With a tip of his hat, he said, "It was certainly a pleasure meeting you two girls. Maybe later we can share a lemonade between card games?" Fritz was only looking at Ruby.

Ruby blushed and smiled. "That would be real nice, Fritz, I look forward to it. It seems like it's going to be a hot day, and perfect for cool lemonade."

Ada felt sparks flying between Fritz and Ruby and quickly cleared her throat. With another tip of his hat, Fritz took Ruby's hand and helped her out of the car. Ruby still had a smile on her face as she and Ada started walking toward the house. "Say, wasn't Fritz a nice fellow?" Ruby asked.

Ada paused. "I thought this was a ladies' party. Why are there gentlemen here?"

Ruby wondered the same thing, but didn't say anything; she was quite smitten by Fritz, and was looking forward to the glass of lemonade promised her later in the day.

The two sisters walked up to the front porch, where the others were standing in the shade underneath the awning. Ada saw that two of the fellows had hair tucked underneath their hats. She could hear one of the gentlemen talking and laughing to a lady standing in front of him. *That's a woman's voice,* she thought. Ada was startled as she realized that both of the fellows standing there were ladies wearing men's clothing. Ada started to grab Ruby's arm to tell her about this discovery, when all of a sudden Cora came out the front door.

"My fine ladies, chums, and pals, I would like to welcome you to my home and thank you all for being here on this beautiful day. Because it's such a glorious day, I've decided to move all the card tables to the backyard so we can take advantage of the first sunny day after our horrible winter. I've also put your names at each of the tables, so you can all have a chance to meet some of the new faces we have here today. So, go find your names and play some cards. The refreshments will be served shortly."

The name tags were not randomly arranged; Cora had an uncanny way of putting the right people together for her card games and parties. She was well known to be quite the matchmaker among her hand-picked group of friends.

Ruby shot off in the direction of the tables, searching for her name. Ada was still standing there, not sure what to think of what was unfolding in front of her. There were four tables, nicely arranged and decorated for the card players. Ruby found her name at the second table and began looking around for her sister's name tag. Ada started walking slowly toward the tables. Ruby didn't notice the concerned look on her sister's face.

"Come on, Ada!" Ruby shouted. "I saw your name at the first table, next to Cora. Come on over and have a seat."

As Ada headed toward the tables, she peered intensely at the features of the other gentlemen card players, including Fritz, and confirmed her suspicions. All the gentlemen were actually ladies dressed as men. Then she started thinking, *Does Cora know about them? Do the other lady card players know about them? Does Ruby know?*

Her head was spinning, and she thought for a moment she might faint. Then one of the lady card players touched her arm and asked if she was feeling unwell. Ada came back to herself and said, "I must not be used to warm weather yet. I think I might need a little water."

Ada found her name tag and sat down while she waited for her water. She needed to be as diplomatic as possible. After all, to leave now would be insulting to Cora, and embarrassing for her and her sister. *There must be a reasonable explanation for all of this,* she thought.

She heard another voice behind her say, "I'll go to the house to get her some water."

Soon Ada was handed a glass of water. The woman smiled and watched Ada take a few careful sips. Ada was still stunned by her revelation, but her breathing was back to normal. She was hoping that the other card players hadn't noticed the perplexed look on her face.

"You look better already," said the woman. "My name is Olga, and you must be Ada."

Ada was puzzled that Olga knew her name. Olga glanced down at the name tag at Ada's seat, and smiled again.

"Oh! How rude of me. Yes, of course, my name is Ada Peterson. So nice to meet you, Olga."

Olga seemed to sense Ada's discomfort. "Say, you've never been to one of Cora's parties before, have you?"

Ada could feel her cheeks blush as she responded, "No, but everyone seems very nice."

Olga leaned toward Ada, and in a very soft Danish accent said, "I'm sure you must have noticed by now that some of the gents here are ladies. But rest assured, they are perfect gentleman. They just prefer to wear the clothing that they are most comfortable with. Although I'm not sure why; it seems much too hot today to be wearing a wool suit and tie." She gave Ada a reassuring smile, which instantly made her feel more comfortable.

Ada asked Olga, "Do they always wear gentlemen's clothing?"

"No, of course not," Olga said with a chuckle. "Most of the ladies here today are schoolteachers, librarians, or nurses. The only time they can wear their gentlemen's clothing is when they come to Cora's or some other 'safe house' for a party." Olga went on to say, "Most people don't care much for ladies in gents' clothing. In fact, a few years ago a teacher in Kansas got hot tar thrown on her by four men after someone in town found out that she liked to dress up as a gent on weekends."

Ada was shocked at what Olga told her. *How could people be so cruel as to pour hot tar on a well-educated lady, or* any *lady, for that matter?*

As everyone found their assigned seats and settled down, Ada was still very aware of the people around her. Olga was sitting to her left and Cora was on her right; one of the chums was sitting across from her. They began playing gin. Ada loved playing cards, so it was easy for her to just concentrate on the game, and she soon forgot about how the women were dressed.

Cora was her usual loud and bossy self, and the others were laughing and having a good time. During the small talk, Ada found out that Olga had graduated from Lawrence University in Appleton and was teaching in Milwaukee. The two of them spent most of the time talking about the upcoming teachers' conference that was going to be held in Milwaukee the next month.

Ada looked at the table where Ruby was sitting and noticed that everyone there was having a jolly time as well. However, she still didn't know if Ruby knew about the true identity of the gentlemen card players yet.

They played cards for over an hour before taking a break. Cora's table was the first to finish, but Ruby's table was still playing. Ada stood behind her sister impatiently, tapping her fingers on the back of Ruby's chair and waiting for her to complete the game so she could tell her everything she'd discovered. As soon as the last card hit the table, she tugged on the back of Ruby's dress. "Come on, sister, let's go get something cool to drink."

Ada wasn't sure if Ruby had any idea that the gentlemen at the party were really ladies, and she didn't want to startle her when she told her. "Did you notice anything odd about Fritz and the other gents here?" she asked her sister.

With a clever smile, Ruby said, "Well, I'm not sure what you mean by odd, but I do know they're all ladies."

Ada was shocked. "Well, Ruby Peterson, how in the world did you figure that out?"

Ruby smiled. "Sister, you may have a teaching degree and I may be younger, but I can certainly figure out some things all on my own. Besides, these gents here are much more interesting than the fellows I know."

Fritz walked by and asked the sisters if they wanted some punch. Ruby looked over her shoulder and said, "That would be marvelous, Fritz. Could you please bring some punch for my sister as well? She seems to be a little parched." Fritz tipped his hat toward the sisters, and proceeded into the house for the punch.

"Now, Ruby Peterson, do not get carried away here. Once we leave this party, we need never speak of this again. You hear me?" This time Ruby was defiant of her sister's commands; she silently turned around and walked toward the house.

Fritz was inside, talking to another chum by the name of Van. Ruby came up and put her hand under Fritz's arm, guiding both of them toward the punchbowl. This took Fritz by surprise. Even Ruby was a little bit surprised by how bold she was being, but she couldn't help herself. From the first moment she met Fritz in the car, and all through the last hour of playing cards, she hadn't been able to take her eyes off him. The flirtation didn't go unnoticed by the other card players at their table, either.

Fritz politely bowed to Ruby. "What would my lady care to drink today, punch or lemonade?"

"I'll have some sweet punch, and I think my sister would like some sour lemonade," Ruby said with a smirk. The remark made Fritz laugh; a deep, rich laugh that filled the room. Ruby couldn't help being drawn in by it.

They were both standing awkwardly, drinking their refreshments, when Fritz looked at Ruby and said, "I don't think your sister approves of me, does she?"

"It's not that she doesn't approve of you, Fritz; she just thinks she's my mother sometimes, and gets carried away. Why would you ask me that?" Ruby asked.

"No reason," Fritz replied. "I think Cora is getting ready to start the second half of the games. We should head back before your sister starts looking for us." Fritz led Ruby back to their chairs.

As the card game and conversations continued, Ada became less and less concerned with the ladies dressed as men. Van, who was sitting across from her, seemed shy, and very much a gentleman. The conversation moved from the suffragette movement to music and theater. She was fascinated by the wide range of topics discussed and how interesting all the ladies were. They were much more engaging than the usual subjects young ladies her age would talk about when they got together.

Once the final round of cards had finished, Ralph, the piano player, started playing ragtime music. Some of the ladies were taking turns dancing with the chums, and with each other. Even Ada found herself compelled to dance with some of the ladies. Everyone seemed so happy and free. She wasn't sure if it was the weather, the music, or the company, but she couldn't remember when she'd had a better time at a party.

Ada was looking for Ruby, and spotted her talking to Fritz underneath one of the huge shade trees in the backyard. They had been there for the last thirty minutes, talking and laughing, and she wondered what they were saying to each other.

As Ada stood on the back porch watching her sister, Olga walked up behind her and peeked over her shoulder.

"So what do you think about all this?"

Ada was startled. "What do you mean, Olga?"

Olga knew that Ada understood what she was talking about, but decided to ask a more detailed question. "About all of these beautiful ladies at the party, and that some of them like to dress as gentleman. What do you think about all this?"

Ada wasn't sure how to respond. "What do I think?"

Olga saved her the agony of having to answer by asking instead, "Well, did you enjoy yourself this afternoon?"

This time the answer was easy for Ada. "Yes, I had a wonderful time."

Olga smiled. "Good. That's all you need to know, and hopefully that's all you need to share with outsiders." The words weren't meant as a threat to Ada; they were only to make her understand that the less outsiders knew about Cora's private parties, the better and safer it would be.

Ada remembered the story about what had happened to the teacher in Kansas, and understood instantly what Olga meant. Ada told Olga that she had no need to share such information with outside people. Their secret was safe with her and her sister. Olga was delighted that Ada didn't seem interested in revealing information about Cora's parties.

Before stepping away, Olga had one more question for Ada. "Say, do you already have your ticket to the teachers' convention in Milwaukee next month?"

Ada's eyes dimmed. "I desperately want to go, but since I just finished my certification I wasn't planning on attending this year."

Olga explained to Ada that she had an extra ticket because one of her coworkers at school would be unable to attend. She told her, "If you're willing to travel into Milwaukee, the ticket is yours."

Ada beamed with excitement. "Oh, Olga, that would be wonderful. I would love to go."

Fritz and Ruby started walking toward Ada and Olga as they were exchanging addresses for the convention. Ada saw that Ruby had her arm underneath Fritz's. When they got close, Ruby told Ada that Fritz would be giving them a ride back home. Ada was not all that pleased, but at the same time, she wasn't surprised about their transportation.

On the way home, Ada sat in the back seat behind Ruby. She noticed that her sister was sitting a little closer to Fritz than she had when they first got picked up on the way to the party. Ruby was also acting like a smitten schoolgirl, giggling at her whispered conversation with Fritz. Fritz could feel Ada's eyes on them both, and nervously glanced over his shoulder at Ada's disapproving stare. Ada was very concerned about how interested Ruby was becoming in Fritz.

Fritz turned right onto Lime Lake Road, drove slowly down the bumpy gravel road, and parked next to the Peterson house. Before Fritz could go around to open the passenger door, Ruby had already jumped out and let her sister out of the back seat. Ada coldly thanked Fritz for the ride home and walked toward their house before Fritz could give her a tip of the hat. Ruby was intrigued by her new friend and decided to stay in the car a little while longer.

Ruby looked at Fritz for a moment and asked what his real name was. Caught off-guard by the question, Fritz took hold of the steering wheel in a steadying grip and looked down. Fritz slowly removed his grip from the wheel and took off the felt bowler hat.

As her long light brown hair unfolded from underneath, she said, "My real name is Elizabeth Fitzgerald, but I prefer to go by Fritz. I know it seems odd, but when I'm dressed as a gent, that's who I am. That's when I feel most myself, instead of being who everyone wants be to be."

With her true identity revealed, Fritz looked uneasy until Ruby reached for her hand. "Elizabeth Fitzgerald is a nice name, but Fritz suits you. Do all the chums have male names like you do?" Ruby asked.

Elizabeth took back her confidence as she pulled on her lapel to straighten her jacket. "Not all of them. Some of the ladies do fancy dressing up as gentlemen occasionally. Me and my pals would dress like this every day if we could."

Ruby's head was swimming with questions, but it was getting late and she felt she was being watched. Before she could say another word, Fritz lifted Ruby's hand and lightly kissed the top of it. "Will I see you again, Ruby?"

She felt Fritz's breath on her hand and heard her own heart pounding in a way she never had before. "Yes, I would like that, Fritz."

There was no kiss between them—only the look in their eyes that promised they would see each other again.

TEN

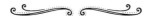

In the early nineteen-hundreds, the suffragette movement was well on its way and groups of women started holding rallies at Camp Cleghorn, about twenty miles from the Peterson farm. There was a lot of anger and resentment from some of the men—and even women—in the surrounding towns, because they still believed that women should not be allowed to vote. They thought women should only focus on being good housewives and mothers, and that politics would confuse them into making bad decisions, either at the polls or at home.

Most people didn't pay much attention to Cora Turner's parties and social events; they assumed it was just a group of young ladies getting together to talk about how they would get married and raise their children someday. But there was some talk in town that those parties were more than just refreshments and card games.

In fact, there were women from as far away as Chicago who would travel by train to attend Cora's parties. It was a way for them to find each other in a world where they knew most people would never understand or accept them. If anyone outside the circle of friends found out how deep their relationships really were, everything would change. They could be forced to marry a man their parents selected, run out of town, put into a mental institution, physically attacked, or even killed. It was dangerous—very dangerous—for them all.

ELEVEN

While doing my research, I found a newspaper article in the *Stevens Point Journal* dated November 22, 1911, about a young female teacher in Kansas by the name of Miss Mary Chamberlin who was ambushed by four men. They grabbed her and pulled her dress over her head, then pushed her to the ground, removed her undergarments, and dumped a bucket of hot tar on her lower body. Then two of the men proceeded to masturbate in front of her, while she was writhing on the ground in excruciating pain from the hot tar.

Three of the men were convicted and given a one-year jail sentence. The other one was acquitted. The article never explained what would motivate these men to do such a horrible thing to this young teacher; however, the symbolism seems apparent. More than likely she had rejected one of them, or they found out why she was not interested in them, and wanted to teach her a lesson.

Not only did this article send chills down my spine because of the brutality, it made me angry at how little jail time the perpetrators received. *Only a year in jail for such a violent crime?* Then I became even angrier when I noticed the article was not front-page news. It wasn't even third-page news! The article was placed in the back of the newspaper, between a piece on the cost of a Thanksgiving dinner and an advertisement for a female kidney pain remedy, which showed a woman bent over an ironing board, holding her back in pain.

Was the article placed there for a reason? Was it a warning to other women? Or did they simply have such little respect for women in general back then? Regardless of the reason, the implications of that article being placed in the back of the paper horrified me to my core.

I discovered a lot of very interesting events and people while doing my research, but that article was by far the most disturbing to me on many levels.

Most of the women in Cora's close circle of friends were well-educated teachers or nurses. These were professions dominated by women at the time. They communicated the dates and times of gatherings with each other by word of mouth or letters, but only with those they trusted. Even when sending letters, they needed to be cautious.

At that time, the U.S. Mail was regularly opened and reviewed by Christian morality groups that advocated legal censorship, like the National Purity Party. The founder of this group was Anthony Comstock, who was also the U.S. postal inspector at that time. The Comstock Act was used from 1874 to the 1940s by social reformers to identify people they believed to be involved in 'immoral or lewd sexual acts,' including homosexuality.

The Comstock Act was originally passed to combat the shipment of pornography and contraception via the U.S. Mail. However, the National Purity Party took a much wider approach when implementing the law: it allowed enforcers the ability to censor personal mail at any time. If found guilty, perpetrators could find themselves facing up to five years hard labor in a state penitentiary, or a fine up to two thousand dollars.

Because of this, it wasn't uncommon for the women to change their names on photos or letters. Often the nicknames they used were abbreviations of their given name. I discovered several photos of my grandmother with the name 'Pete' printed underneath, probably short for Peterson.

It was a very dangerous time for them all. When these women were together, it was so electrifying that any fear of retribution left them. But still, the danger was always there.

BARES TARRING PLOT

KANSAN ADMITS CLOTHES WERE TORN FROM YOUNG SCHOOL TEACHER.

RUB PITCH ON NAKED BODY

Chester Anderson's Tale of How Mary Chamberlain Was Trapped by Men of Shady Bend and Mistreated.

Bad Kidneys—Weak Back—Weary Woman

Dr. Derby's Guaranteed Kidney Pills Make Such Women Happy—Ward Off Old Age—Try Them Free!

SUCCESSFUL COLLECTOR.

TWELVE

While at Cora's party, Ruby felt as if a dark cloud around her had been suddenly lifted. She didn't feel the need to act like someone she wasn't. There was no need for her to pretend she was looking for a suitable husband, or to talk about starting a family someday. In the last two years, at every party she attended, her family and friends would ask her the same dreaded question: "When are you going to find a nice fellow, get married and have children?" Clearly that was not a topic of conversation at Cora's party.

At first, Ruby was a little startled when she figured out for herself that the gentlemen at Cora's party were all women. However, she felt comfort and acceptance within the group. When Ruby was talking to Fritz, she found out that there was a network of women who felt the same way she did. Most of them lived in big cities like Chicago, New York, or Los Angeles, and there were several 'safe locations' in the surrounding towns as well. However, the women preferred visiting smaller towns, because the National Purity Party spent less time looking for 'immoral' behavior in rural areas.

Ruby now knew she wasn't the only one with these thoughts and feelings toward other women. It was all starting to come into focus for her, much like taking a photograph and watching the picture develop. She realized that these successful, happy, smart women didn't need or want a husband in their lives. They had found love and companionship with each other, in a way Ruby had only dreamt about.

When the sisters came home from Cora's party that evening, Ada watched Ruby and Fritz from the house. Her initial shock at the women dressed in men's clothing had disappeared. She was far more concerned that Ruby's interest in the ladies might be more than curiosity. Ada did not talk to her sister about what transpired at the party when they got home; she was hoping it was merely an interesting event that they would both soon forget.

But Ada noticed a change in Ruby after the party. Her sister seemed happier than she had been in ages. She even offered to do extra chores around the house, something that up to that point Ruby had hardly ever done. Ada wondered if Fritz, or the other ladies at the party, had anything to do with Ruby's newfound happiness.

A week after the party, the sisters were walking out to the barn for their morning chore of milking the cows. The sun was just cresting over the hillside, and they could hear the frost crackling on the ground as they walked. They really didn't mind going to the barn that early, because often it was warmer there than in the house.

Before entering the barn, Ruby stopped and stood outside to feel the sun on her face growing warmer. She hated getting up so early, but that morning she decided it was her favorite part of the day. As she watched the sky turn a lighter shade of blue, she could hear the birds beginning to chirp in the background. It seemed that the world was ready to celebrate the new day with her.

With milk bucket in hand, Ada walked up behind Ruby and said, "Say, you've been in good spirits lately. How come?"

Ruby looked surprised, but she'd actually been expecting Ada's question, or at least a comment about her changed disposition.

"What do you mean, sister? I'm just enjoying the sunrise on this glorious day."

Ada was irritated by Ruby's vague answer, and stepped into the barn. Ruby closed her eyes one last time to feel the sun on her face before tending to the cows.

For over ten minutes there was awkward silence between the sisters. Ruby knew Ada was frustrated with her answer, but honestly, she wasn't sure how or what to tell her. She only knew that something wonderful had happened at Cora's party.

How could I possibly explain all of this? she thought.

Ruby finally broke the silence by asking Ada if she wanted to go to town at the end of the week. She knew they always had their best times together when they were window-shopping and catching up on the town gossip.

Ada understood that whatever was going on with Ruby, she wasn't ready to talk about it yet. Maybe the trip into town would do them both some good. Ada smiled. "Sure, sister, that would be fun. But we must get all of our chores done before Daddy comes home, or we won't be able to go."

THIRTEEN

August 1914

The first of Cora's parties the sisters attended was not their last. Ada and Ruby went to several more parties over the next four months, though they each had very different reasons for doing so.

Ada enjoyed the stimulating conversations with other well-educated women about teaching, art, and politics—something she had desperately missed after leaving college. Since her return to the farm, she found that almost no young ladies her age were willing to speak of such things, and gentleman callers would not take kindly to such 'inappropriate' talk by a woman.

There was no romantic motive for Ada to attend Cora's parties; they were simply an outlet to keep her mind open. In the process, she formed deep friendships with many of the 'ladies and chums.' It was also a way of keeping a watchful eye on her younger sister. Ada was concerned that Ruby's involvement with some of the chums was more than platonic, and she wanted to make sure her younger sister was kept out of harm's way. On the other hand, it was the first time she had seen Ruby so happy, and since all the ladies were respectable, no harm would probably come from it all. *As long as nobody gets caught,* she thought.

It had been months since Ruby had seen Fritz, yet the time they spent flirting with each other was never far from her thoughts. Every party she attended, her eyes scoured the room without success, until she decided she could wait no more. She searched the room to find someone who might know whereabouts of the elusive 'Mr. Fritz.' She finally saw Van, and asked in a nonchalant tone, "Where has Fritz been? I haven't seen your pal in ages."

Van could hardly say the words, and looked down to choke back tears. In a soft cracking voice he said, "Fritz is gone."

Ruby was beside herself. "Gone! What do you mean, gone?"

Van explained to Ruby, "When Fritz got home from Cora's party the evening you met, she was told by her mother and father that she was to marry the son of a successful businessman in town."

Ruby's heart sank to a depth she'd never felt before. "Please, Van, you must tell me where I can find her."

"I don't know where she is, or how to find her, Ruby. I believe she left town for good."

Ruby was desperate for answers. "Is she going to marry the fellow?"

"No," Van said. "She always swore that if her parents ever imposed marriage she would move to New York, or maybe Los Angeles. I believe that's where she's gone. Fritz also told me that if that were to happen, no one should come looking for her, because she would never allow herself to be found."

Ruby was relieved to hear that Fritz would not surrender into marriage, but was heartbroken knowing she would never see him again.

After such news, Ruby was no longer interested in being at the party. She began looking for her sister so they could start the long walk home. She found Ada talking to a chum she had never seen before. The chum was wearing the typical gentleman's suit and black bowler.

She hesitated to interrupt their conversation, but her head was swimming with grief and she felt she had to leave. "Sister, I'd like to go home now. I've got a terrible headache."

Being interrupted mid-sentence by her sister visibly annoyed Ada. "Ella, let me formally introduce you to my younger sister, Ruby, who is not normally so rude."

Ella tipped her hat toward Ruby as Ada continued the introduction. "Ruby, this is Ella Karnopp. She graduated from Lawrence University last year and will be teaching high school in Sheboygan this fall."

Ruby was not impressed, and still more interested in going home, but didn't want to be as rude as her sister suggested.

"My pleasure to meet you, Ruby. I've heard a lot about you. I'm sorry you're not feeling well this evening."

Ruby responded, "You must be new to Cora's parties. I haven't seen you before."

"Actually, I'm not really new here. I've just been out of town for the last six months, traveling," Ella said.

Ruby's eyes lit up when she heard that Ella had been traveling, and suddenly she wanted to hear more. "That sounds wonderful, Ella. Where did you travel to?"

"After graduation, I took the train to the West Coast to see some of my family and friends. However, it was a much shorter trip than I planned for. In fact, I had hoped to get a new teaching position and move there permanently."

Ruby had never met anyone before who had traveled to the West Coast. The farthest she had ever been was to Milwaukee to visit her aunt and uncle for holidays. The only things she really knew about the West were what she'd read in the newspapers or seen in plays at the local opera house.

"Did you run into any Indians out there?" Ruby asked jokingly.

Ella chuckled and answered Ruby's question. "Heavens no, my dear, everyone is quite civilized. In fact, you would be amazed how nice folks are, and how beautiful the Pacific Ocean is. You must go if you ever have the opportunity to do so."

Ruby's headache was starting to dissipate, and she was intrigued to find out more about Ella and her recent travels. "Is there another name you'd prefer to go by?"

Ella was surprised by Ruby's bold question and appreciated her concern, given her suit and tie. "For now you can call me by my given name," Ella said with a smile.

"Did you travel all the way to the West on the train by yourself?"

Ella's expression turned to stone, and she answered grimly, "Yes, I did, even though I purchased two tickets."

Ruby sensed another story, but judging from the look on Ella's face and her response, she didn't want to pursue any more questions about her trip to the West.

Ella abruptly tipped her hat toward the sisters and said, "Ada and Ruby, it was a pleasure meeting you both, but it's getting late and I promised my brothers I would be home for dinner. Ruby, I hope you feel better. Good evening." Then she walked away.

Ada looked at Ruby as if she'd done something to offend Ella. Ruby immediately defended herself. "Now sister, you know I only asked if she had traveled to the West by herself. Besides, she seemed awfully snooty. And what did she mean she's heard a lot about me?"

Ada rolled her eyes. "Ruby, you're so nosy. Why do you always have to ask so many questions? Anyway, I thought you had a headache. Let's get going, then. I'm sure Leroy has been waiting for us to fix his supper."

The early evening breeze was warm, and crickets were chirping in perfect unison as the sisters left the party. A small group of ladies and chums were standing on Cora's front porch, sipping lemonade and talking. Ruby wasn't trying to eavesdrop, but she couldn't help overhearing that they were talking about going camping next month.

Ruby tugged on Ada's sleeve. "Did you hear that? They want to go on a camping trip." Ada had heard her, but was desperately hoping her sister hadn't, because she knew Ruby loved to camp.

Ruby couldn't contain herself. "I know a grand place to go camping, and it's not that far from here," she called to the group. "They have cottages and tents to rent, and it has some of the best fishing and canoeing around. It's called Camp Cleghorn."

Ada pulled on the back of Ruby's dress and whispered, "I thought you weren't feeling well, sister? Why are you planning a camping trip with the ladies now?"

Ruby ignored her sister's tugging and continued talking. After she was done telling the girls about Camp Cleghorn, she abruptly turned to face her sister. "Ada, why do you keep pulling on my dress? I'm just telling the girls where we can all go camping."

"Ruby, you know I'm going to Milwaukee next month. I can't possibly go camping with you," Ada said.

Ruby was defiant. "Ada, there's no need for you to go camping with me and the girls. I'm sure we can manage to have a jolly time without you there."

Ruby was fully aware that her sister was keeping a watchful eye over her, but she felt it was time for her to start socializing on her own.

FOURTEEN

The last time Grandma Ruby was at Camp Cleghorn I was standing by her side. She was sixty-nine years old; I was only four. I don't remember being there, but I found a newspaper clipping from 1965 that my grandma had saved in her treasure box of memories. The article told about a family reunion that was held at Camp Cleghorn that summer. It had a picture of my mother, Grandma Ruby, an uncle and aunt, two cousins, and me. We were all standing in front of a little white cottage next to the lake.

When I looked at the photograph, I couldn't help wondering what Grandma Ruby was thinking about at the time. As she stood on the rocky shore next to the crystal-clear lake, did she smile when she recalled the camping trip that had taken place there over fifty years ago? When she gazed at the trees and rocks that surrounded her, did she dream for a moment she was eighteen years old again? Was she remembering all the wonderful things that happened there?

FIFTEEN

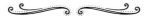

1914

In the summer of 1914, Ruby helped to organize a weekend camping trip with eight of the ladies and chums. The gals decided to rent tents there, rather than carrying them to the side of the lake themselves. These were not the standard tents we use today: they were more like small houses made out of heavy canvas, with tall wooden poles for support. Once a tent was erected, five people could stand in the middle with no need to bend over.

Camp Cleghorn was only about twenty miles from where Ruby lived, and she managed to get a ride there from one of her neighbors. Since it was the first event Ruby had helped organize, she wanted to get there first to ensure it was set up properly and that the location of their campsite was perfect. Once she got there, she walked among the evergreens and Norway pine trees, then stopped and stood for a moment with her hands on her hips. As she was enjoying the solitude of the forest, she noticed a clearing next to the lake. It was far enough from the other campsites that outsiders wouldn't be close enough to wonder why a group of women were camping without a man around to help them. She smiled, because she knew she had found the perfect spot. She walked back up to the general store and waited for one of the groundskeepers to help set up the tents. The groundskeeper wasn't happy when Ruby told him where she wanted the tents erected, because it wasn't along the standard path of other campsites. However, Ruby used her charm and promised a good tip in return.

Once all four tents were set up, Ruby sat on a tree stump waiting for the gals to arrive. Almost two hours had gone by, and she was starting to get worried that they couldn't find her or had gotten lost on the way. However, soon she heard the unmistakable laughter of Cora and the girls.

Ruby shouted out, "Hey, I'm over here!" She could hear the small, thin branches snapping as the gals started running through the trees toward her.

Cora spotted Ruby and yelled out, "Olly-olly-oxen everyone is free!"

Ruby bent over laughing. "Cora, I don't think there could possibly be an animal or fish that couldn't hear you from ten miles away. What took you gals so long to get here?"

Moments later, five other campers dashed out of the forest like a bunch of wild deer. Out scampered Maude and Frances, Sara and Bessie, and then Drake.

Cora, out of breath and with twigs stuck in her blonde mane from running through the forest, was holding onto the side of one of the pine trees for support. "Ruby, do you not understand how difficult it is to fit all these women and their bags into one car?"

Ruby was still laughing. "Cora, do you mean to tell me that all of you had to come here in one car?"

Cora was chuckling now too. "No, we didn't have to, but it seemed like the most fun way to do it."

Once Ruby and Cora stopped laughing, Ruby did a headcount and noticed one of the chums was missing. "Say, what happened to Harriet? Did she fall out of the car on the way up?"

"No," said one of the girls. "She got called into the hospital to work this weekend, but one of her pals from school will be joining us instead. She's driving in from her brother's house in Almond and should be here any time."

The gals started putting their things away, and Ruby noticed as they paired up into three of the tents. She was the only person to have a tent to herself. "Hey, what am I going to do? I don't have anyone to talk to at night. I'm over here by myself."

Drake stepped out of the tent, still tucking in an oversized white shirt into a pair of brown men's trousers which looked to be five sizes too large. Her long blonde hair had already been pulled back into a ponytail and tucked cleanly under a big white floppy straw hat. As Drake was pulling up the suspenders to keep her pants from falling down, she said, "Don't worry, Ruby, we won't let any bears eat ya out here. Ella should be here soon, she'll protect you."

Ruby thought for a moment. *Please don't let it be that Ella —the snooty Ella that I got in trouble with Ada over.* She had to know. "Is that the Ella that's going to start teaching high school in Sheboygan this fall?"

Drake thought about it for a moment. "Yes, I believe it is. I think she also goes by the name O'Brien occasionally, and recently returned from the West Coast after her lady refused to move there with her. Poor chum."

Ruby knew it was the same Ella, and was now dreading her perfect camping weekend. Also, she understood now why Ella had reacted to her question about traveling alone the way she did. Even though she wasn't pleased to learn who her tent-mate for the weekend was, she was determined to make the best of it.

All of a sudden, Cora popped out of her tent and announced, "This place will now and forever be called Camp Cora." She proceeded to hang a pair of ladies' bloomers on a pole outside her tent like a flag.

Before Ella arrived, Ruby changed into clothing that was suitable for romping around in the woods. She took pictures of the gals as they climbed trees and rocks by the lake, all of them laughing and having the best time. Ruby stopped to skip a few rocks into the crystal-clear water of Dake Lake. As she watched the ripples fade away, she closed her eyes and wished the day would never end.

By the time they got back to camp, Ella had arrived and was sitting on a boulder reading a book beneath the shade of a large pine tree. She was wearing a heavy black wool suit, and didn't look at all comfortable.

Ruby saw Ella and was dreading meeting her again, but figured she would do her best to be pleasant. She certainly had no intention of bringing up anything about her trip to the West Coast. Drake hollered out, "Say, old pal, what are you doing just sitting there looking like a lump on a rock?"

Ella looked up from her book, seemingly unamused, and responded in a serious manner, "I suppose I wanted to make sure this was the right camp spot before getting too comfortable out here in the middle of the forest. However, since I saw someone's bloomers hanging on top of that tent pole, I figured this must be the place. Either that, or someone was trying to scare the bears away."

With her hands on her hips, Cora shouted toward Ella, "For your information, Ella, those are my bloomers, and they were made in France from the finest silk. They also happen to be our official Camp Cora flag."

Ella could no longer hold back her laughter as Cora approached to greet her with a big hug and a kiss on her cheek. Ruby enjoyed seeing evidence of Ella's wit and dry sense of humor. Maybe spending the weekend with her wouldn't be so bad after all.

Even though Ella had sworn off meeting another lady after the last one left her heart broken, she was looking forward to spending time with her pals at Camp Cleghorn, now known as Camp Cora. She saw Ruby standing there and realized she needed to apologize for her abrupt exit when they first met. She also knew she needed to guard against being attracted to Ruby. She wasn't ready to leave herself vulnerable again, not for anyone.

Ella walked up to Ruby, tipped her hat, and said, "Miss Ruby, it's a pleasure to meet you again. I'm sorry for my dreadful behavior when we met previously. I had just returned home the day before and I'm afraid I was still tired from the long train ride. I hope you will forgive me."

Ruby pretended not to know what she was referring to. "Oh, that," she said. "It's quite all right, Ella. I wasn't feeling well myself that evening. I had just found out that a friend of mine moved far away and I would likely never see her again."

With that, Ella removed her hat and allowed her long dark hair to fall to her shoulders. "I suppose we both know that horrible feeling of never seeing someone that we care deeply about again."

Ruby smiled and said, "I suppose we do."

For the rest of the weekend at 'Camp Cora,' the women enjoyed the freedom of living in their own little protected world. Drake managed to catch a good amount of largemouth bass, and the ladies prepared a daily outdoor feast. During the day, they spent time canoeing and swimming in the lake. At night, they sat around the campfire telling jokes and laughing, and occasionally breaking out into song. For that weekend, it was their perfect world—a world in which they didn't need to hide.

During the weekend camping trip, Ella and Ruby spent a great deal of time with each other and developed a friendship. Usually, after the others had gone to bed, the two of them would spend hours talking and laughing about different people and events in their lives. Ruby moved her cot closer to Ella's so the campers in the other tents couldn't hear who or what they were talking about. Ella eventually told Ruby why she had gone to the West Coast alone. She explained that she had purchased two tickets to Portland, Oregon, and that one of the tickets had been for the woman she loved. They'd planned on moving there together to start a new life, but instead the woman was forced by her parents to marry a man they selected.

The last night before going home, Ella warned Ruby, "Let me tell you, the life we lead is not an easy one. There are many dangers in the world for us—it's dangerous if other people find out, because of what they might do to us. Some will want to hurt us or put us into mental institutions. Some want to get rid of us altogether. Others will try to 'cure' us by forcing us into marriage, thinking that all we need is a 'good man.' Let me assure you, sweet lady, there is no cure for what ails us, because we are not ill."

Ella was telling Ruby this, not to scare her, but to make sure she knew fully what she was getting into. However, for Ella there was nothing more dangerous than a woman who would succumb to the pressure of her parents.

First photo -Ruby (second from the left) camping with the gals

Ruby – Who is Coming?   *Ruby Rowing*

Ruby on the rocks (on the left)

*Ruby up a tree
(on the right)*

SIXTEEN

Amherst 2014

There was a long list of things I wanted to do on my first trip to Amherst. I carefully strategized my week ahead of time by planning multiple tasks each day, much as I would do when getting ready for a big meeting or project at my job. I didn't know it at the time, but my list of things to do would quickly fall by the wayside once I got there.

One of the important items on my list was to find the headstones of my great-grandparents, Peter and Hilda Peterson. I spent the better part of one full day searching two cemeteries located just outside of town, and found nothing. I decided to make my way to the larger cemetery at the edge of town. As I drove through the wrought-iron front gate of Greenwood Cemetery, I noticed immediately how much larger it was compared to the graveyards I had visited earlier that day—almost three city blocks. Clearly, I needed to be much more calculating in my approach when looking for my family.

I started in the first section by the front entrance and noticed that most of the headstones there were newer, with recent death dates. Some even had fresh-cut flowers which hadn't yet wilted, and paths carved in the grass by frequent visitors. I changed direction and started walking to the far end of the cemetery, hoping to find the older grave markers—the ones so old time had forgotten them.

As I walked, I could tell by the dates on the weathered stones that my instinct was correct. The older section of the cemetery was well-maintained, but not like the newer section. There were no flower arrangements left on any of these headstones; only clumps of crabgrass growing between the markers from years without visitors.

I suppose it's natural to start questioning one's own mortality when walking in a cemetery. It was so quiet that I could hear the breeze darting in and out of the tree limbs above me, and an occasional squirrel scurrying through the dried leaves looking for nuts. Reaching the older part of the grounds, I noticed some of the people had passed away more than a hundred years ago. It was sad, wondering when had been the last time anyone had spoken their name or even thought of them. I realized that would happen to me someday, and to my family and friends. Eventually time would erase us all... But how long does it take for our existence to completely disappear? Is it fifty or sixty years? Is it more? Or worse, is it less?

Even after I pushed my dismal thoughts away, I was becoming frustrated and a little disappointed at not finding what I came there to find. I was falling behind on my schedule for the day. Not to mention I would be running out of light in the next few hours, and the grumbling in my stomach told me it would be time for dinner soon. Feeling defeated, hungry, and tired, it occurred to me that I might not find what I was looking for.

Just as I was about to give up hope, I saw a large headstone at the far corner of the cemetery with a big 'P' etched into it. I was drawn to it, hoping my vision wasn't playing tricks on me and that my mission for the day would soon be completed. As I walked closer, I was able to make out the name 'Peterson' underneath the large engraved initial. I had found it—the Peterson family plot. I was so happy that all of my prior morbid thoughts and hunger pains disappeared instantly, and I hollered out, "There you are! I've been looking for you everywhere." There were smaller headstones on either side of the larger one. There they were: Peter, Hilda, Eddie, and Leroy Peterson. Grandma Ruby was missing because she was buried in St. Louis.

I stood there for a while, overwhelmed with my find, and thinking I was done for the day. Now the cemetery seemed to come alive with my thoughts of them. I envisioned my Great-Grandfather Peter standing there, holding his pipe in one hand, with the thumb of his other hand tucked underneath his suspenders. My great-grandmother, Hilda, looking up from reading the weekly Gazette and saying to me, "California? You came here all the way from California just to see us?"

Chills ran down my spine as I started cleaning the dust and dirt from their headstones and pulled some weeds that had grown in between them. I hoped they would be pleased knowing that they had not been forgotten after so many years. I began saying my goodbyes, and took a few photos. When I turned to my left to leave I saw the headstone for Alfred and Christina Anderson, my other great-grandparents.

Finding both sets of my great-grandparents was more than I could have hoped for. Every name I saw was of a person I had done research on, and now they were real. The memories of all of them were very much alive inside me. It was a crazy and wonderful family reunion of sorts. I sensed that my visit was a pleasant sort of surprise party for everyone; I laughed out loud at the surreal moment.

I spent the next couple of hours cleaning my family's headstones and saying my prayers and goodbyes. With a twinge of sadness, I turned to walk away. After that, I decided that going forward, my journey would be led by the love of my ancestors, not my list of 'things to do.'

Little did I know I would make yet another discovery before leaving the cemetery that late afternoon.

SEVENTEEN

As I left the cemetery feeling loved by the family I'd never met, something caught my eye. I must have walked by it two or three times before it called me over. It was a very small white marble headstone, about the same size and shape as a shoebox. The grave marker was out of place compared to the other large, weathered gray stones, and the six-foot border of ground around it suggested that the person had no family to be buried alongside. Maybe that's why I felt so compelled to pay it a visit.

As I walked up to the lonesome little headstone, I could see the simple Art Nouveau accent underneath the name. It belonged to Cora Turner (1865-1953). I lost my breath and almost dropped my camera. I knew very well who Cora Turner was; I had come across her name many times in the newspapers, and had already done a fair amount of research on her. This modest little headstone belonged to one of the most flamboyant and progressive women in town.

Most people who lived in and around the Amherst and Stevens Point area in the early 1900s knew Cora Turner, or at least knew of her. Her mother passed away when she was a young girl, and her father spent most of his time away in Massachusetts running a highly successful steel business. Being an only child in a privileged family allowed her luxuries that most people in the area didn't have. However, Cora was also a smart businesswoman and accrued most of her wealth through her own lucrative business investments.

Along with financial wealth, she also had a lot of influence over local politicians and business owners. People didn't dare question why she had never taken a husband. Instead, men would usually joke that Cora was too smart to get married, and the ladies in town would say she was too loud, and no man would put up with her.

Little did any of them know that Cora never had any interest in being married to a man. If they did, they knew it was best to keep such thoughts to themselves. People usually described her as being eccentric, maybe because of her generous financial contributions to the area, including the town library and local schools. Cora embraced that title and wore it like a badge of honor, because it allowed her the independence she desired.

Cora was famous for her elaborate dinner parties, and made it a point to invite local politicians, leading businessmen, and even church leaders from surrounding towns. Invitations to Cora's parties were eagerly accepted by the who's-who in the area, and attendees surely expected to be entertained in high style, using only the finest china and silk table décor.

Less well known, of course, were her private parties with a hand-selected group of lady friends. Along with being a shrewd and influential businesswoman, Cora knew how to hide in plain sight. She figured out quickly that people of influence would be less inclined to pay attention to any unfavorable rumors about her, or her 'woman-only' parties, if they too were frequent guests to her home.

Cora was not concerned for her own safety as much as she was for her 'ladies and chums,' as she would call them. In more ways than one, invitations to her exclusive parties were always risky. Most of the women were well-educated, and employed as teachers, nurses, or librarians. They could easily lose their livelihoods if discovered, and would face public humiliation and scorn. Cora worked hard over the years to establish a trusted and safe environment in which they could enjoy each other's company. After all, nervous houseguests made for horrible parties, and Cora loved nothing more than a good party.

As I stood over her modest headstone, all I could think was, *What a small memorial for a larger-than-life woman.*

Or maybe that's how Cora wanted it. She spent her entire life hiding in plain sight and providing a safe place for her 'ladies and chums.' When I got home, I did additional research and found out that Cora was a member of the International Association of Rebekah Assemblies. The Daughters of Rebekah, also known as the Rebekahs, is an international service-oriented organization and a branch of the Independent Order of Odd Fellows.

It all made sense once I read the Rebekah Creed:

I AM A REBEKAH:

I believe in the Fatherhood of God, the Brotherhood of man, and the Sisterhood of women.

I believe in the watch-words of our Order—Friendship, Love, and Truth.

Friendship—is like a golden chain that ties our hearts together. Love—is one of our most precious gifts, the more you give, the more you receive. Truth—is the standard by which we value people. It is the foundation of our society.

I believe that my main concern should be my God, my family and my friends. Then I should reach out to my community and the World, for in God's eyes we are all brothers and sisters.

I AM A REBEKAH.

With this discovery, I had a clear understanding why Cora did what she did. I believed she lived the Rebekah Creed by protecting those who could not find love otherwise. Although most people at that time would say that her ladies and chums were not God's will, she knew that in God's eyes love is truly one of our most precious gifts; one which needs protection. Cora was the protector of love.

EIGHTEEN

Over the next couple of months after the infamous camping trip, Ella and Ruby attended several of Cora's parties together. Everyone could see how smitten they had become with each other, but they were each too afraid to act on their feelings.

One Saturday evening in September, Ella was invited to the Peterson home for dinner. With her father out of town for a few days, there was only Leroy to take care of, and Ruby wanted to make the most of her extra freedom.

There was a flurry of activity in the kitchen. Ruby had spent all day cooking, and even talked Leroy into catching some fish for dinner that evening. There was a chill in the air outside, but the kitchen felt like the middle of summer because the wood-burning stove was working overtime for the occasion.

Ruby laid out the tapestry tablecloth her mother had made, which was normally only used for Thanksgiving or Christmas dinners. She pushed back the hair and sweat on her forehead with her sleeve as she placed the best family dishes on the table. She smiled, thinking how pleased her mother would be to see her setting such a fine dinner table.

Ruby had picked a handful of white and yellow wildflowers she found next to the lake earlier that day and put them in a Mason jar as a table decoration. As the aroma of home cooking was starting to permeate the house, she heard the sound of a car engine in the distance.

All the activity in the house came to a stop. Ruby ran to look out the dining-room window and saw a cloud of dust trailing behind the approaching car. She hoped it was her dinner guest. Her hopes were soon confirmed when she saw Ella bouncing toward the house wearing a black suit, hat, and driving gloves.

She waved and smiled at Ella from inside the house as she drove past, but Ella was too deep in thought to notice. She parked her car close to the barn so that it wouldn't be seen by unexpected company, and so it would be easy enough to leave quickly, if necessary. Ruby heard the car engine sputter and wheeze as it was turned off and waited for Ella to get out so she could wave her into the house. After almost five minutes there was still no movement from the car. Ruby wasn't sure what to think.

Ruby was becoming concerned that Ella had taken ill. Just as she was starting to pull away from the window to check on her dinner guest, the driver's door slowly opened. Ella was wearing what looked to be a new black suit. Ruby noticed she had a stoic look on her face. She recalled that look from the first time she'd met Ella, and thought something must be terribly wrong. Ella slowly removed her driving gloves and stood motionless for a moment before reaching into the back seat for something. Then, with a quick movement, Ella pulled out the largest bouquet of flowers Ruby had ever seen. Ruby's heart raced at the sight and she felt a blush start to heat her face.

Ruby's eyes widened as she quickly hid behind the curtain, hoping Ella had not seen her. She looked around the dining room and kitchen, not knowing what to think or what to do next. She noticed the Mason jar of small, gangly flowers and quickly ran over and picked it up. Water splashed everywhere as she hid the flowers in a cabinet next to the kitchen.

Ruby glanced around one more time to make sure everything was perfectly set for dinner, then ran to the front door to let Ella in. She opened the door quickly, but Ella was nowhere to be seen. Then she heard a knock at the back door and ran to answer it. By the time she got there she was out of breath, and flushed from the heat of the kitchen and the excitement of seeing the flowers Ella had brought her.

As she opened the door, Ruby tried to pretend that she hadn't been running around the house for the last few minutes like a chicken with her head cut off. "Welcome to my humble abode, Ella. Please come in," she said, trying to be funny.

Ella had been to the Peterson home before, but never for dinner. Ella looked at Ruby standing there: her hair was a bit of a mess, probably from cooking all day, and there was a small dab of flour on the right side of her face. Still, Ella couldn't help but think how beautiful she looked.

She hid the flowers behind her back, feeling too shy to give them to Ruby just yet. She pretended to be very formal as well, speaking with her best fake British accent. She bowed and tipped her new hat. "Lady Ruby, splendid to see you, my dear. I hope you don't mind, but I took the liberty of bringing some flowers for the table."

Ruby, of course, acted surprised when she saw them. "Oh, Ella, they're beautiful. Thank you! I'm so glad you brought them. I didn't have anything to decorate the table."

Ella couldn't resist and said, "Say, it looks like you brought me some beautiful flour as well."

Ruby was confused about what Ella meant, and looked around. "What do you mean, Ella? I don't have any flowers for you."

Ella started laughing and wiped the flour from Ruby's cheek. "This was the flour I was referring to, Ruby."

Ruby blushed, both from finding out she had flour on her face and from Ella's soft touch on her cheek as she removed it.

DON'T YOU DARE

When Ella pulled up to Ruby's house for dinner, she sat in her car praying that this time would be different. Unlike most of the women at Cora's parties, Ella didn't have the same kind of pressures the others did. Although she had two older brothers and a sister, both of Ella's parents were deceased, which alleviated much of the threat of imposed marriage. Still, when she pulled up to Ruby's house for dinner, she questioned herself. *Does Ruby have the strength to fully commit to a relationship with me? Will she leave to marry a man like the others? Can I endure another lost love?*

Even as she removed her driving gloves outside of Ruby's home, she told herself, *It's not too late to turn around and drive away.* But there was another part of her that couldn't walk away from Ruby and what could be. Reaching for the flowers in the back of her car and walking toward Ruby was the equivalent of jumping into the Niagara Falls headfirst, without knowing how to swim.

ᐯᐯ

Ruby reached for one of her mother's large decorative vases for the flowers and arranged them on the table while Ella sat on the couch reading a past edition of the weekly gazette. It was old news, but she needed to read something to keep her mind off of how nervous and exposed she felt giving Ruby flowers. The aroma of food cooking on the stove reminded her how hungry she was, and how much she missed the smell of her mother's cooking. However, her memory was soon interrupted by the smell of something burning.

Ruby smelled it too and ran over to the oven. "Oh, heavens no. My bread is burning!" She opened the oven door and was relieved to find that only one of the corners of the two loaves was burnt. She noticed that the loaves had expanded while baking and touched each other, now becoming fused together on one side. As she was taking them out of the oven, she said to Ella, "Look, it's kissing-crust."

She looked down and blushed after she said it, hoping that Ella understood the meaning behind it. Ruby's remark did not go unnoticed by

Ella. She stood next to Ruby for a moment, looking at her, before leaning over to kiss her. In that moment, a soft kiss changed everything.

Ruby stood motionless for a moment. Even though she was hoping for a kiss from Ella, the sensation of having another woman's lips on hers was foreign. She was amazed how soft Ella felt. She could feel a warm tingle running up her spine, and she knew Ella was looking at her. There was a question in Ella's eyes, asking if her kiss was welcomed.

For Ella, the moment seemed to last forever. She held her breath in anticipation of Ruby's response, fearing that by making such a bold move she had jeopardized their friendship. She was also worried that allowing herself to act on her feelings made her vulnerable to heartbreak, but she was willing to sacrifice her fear for love.

Once the rush of the moment left her, Ruby looked at Ella and smiled. The smile told Ella that she was not alone in her desires for a closer relationship. With both of them now blushing, Ella broke the silence. "My lord, it's hot in this kitchen. Do you have anything cool to drink?"

"I just made some lemonade this afternoon. Let me go pour you a glass."

As she reached into the cooler box to get the lemonade, Ruby missed the relieved look on Ella's face. Before handing the glass to Ella, Ruby leaned in and kissed her this time.

Ella was surprised by Ruby's kiss, which was both more passionate and familiar. Ruby stepped back and said, "We should have dinner now, before it gets cold."

Ella nodded in agreement, feeling as if the temperature in the kitchen was now two hundred degrees. Ruby rushed to bring the rest of the food to the table, and before she could be seated Ella pulled out her chair. "Mademoiselle, please let me do the honors."

The two of them sat for a moment in silence. Ella could hear her heart pounding, and she loosened her shirt collar to speak. "This is a lovely dinner, Ruby. I can't remember when someone has prepared a better meal for me."

"Thank you, Ella. I hope the bread isn't too crispy for you. I normally don't let it bake that long."

"I'm quite pleased you did," Ella said with a shy grin.

Ella and Ruby retired to the parlor after dinner and were soon joined by Leroy, who had spent the afternoon at a friend's house down the road. He ran into the house waving the newspaper wildly over his head. "Take a look at this, will ya—Germany invaded France and thousands of people are dead. I hope those dirty Germans don't come over here. If they do, I'll blow the heads off of every last one a' them."

Leroy was so upset about what he'd read he didn't notice they had a houseguest. "Say, what smells so good?" he asked as he headed toward the kitchen.

Ruby felt her face flush as she cleared her throat. "Excuse me, Leroy. Before you start gobbling your supper, there is someone very special I'd like you to meet."

Ruby ignored his eye-roll and shot him a look telling him to mind his manners. "Leroy, this is my best friend Ella. She teaches German studies at Sheboygan High School, and she's here to join me for dinner tonight."

Ruby watched Leroy's eyes narrow and braced herself to explain Ella's attire. However, before Ruby could utter a word, Leroy asked Ella, "What kind of teacher are you?"

Ella was quick to respond. "I teach German studies to my students. It's important for young people to understand many different parts of the world if they are to have a well-rounded education."

Ruby watched as Leroy studied Ella and his eyes narrowed even more. "Say, are you one of those Germans?"

Ella had become accustomed to explaining her teachings since the war had erupted in Europe, and stood resolved when answering Leroy's question. "It is true that my parents and I immigrated to the United States from Germany when I was only a baby, and I have many uncles and aunts who still live there. It's been months since I've heard from any of them, and I fear for their safety."

Leroy's face was red-hot and his fists were clenched. Ruby had never seen him act that way, and for a moment feared what her younger brother might do. "Are they fighting in the war over there?" he asked abruptly.

Ella heard the hatred and anger in Leroy's throat and responded, "Good heavens, no! They are much too old for that, but if they were doing battle, I'm sure they would be fighting against the Kaiser and not with him. You see, not all Germans like him: that's because he and his family turned a once-beautiful country into a nation of hate, and proud people into cowards. That's why I teach the poetry, music, and folklore of a once-magnificent country. America is our home now, and we will fight to protect it. Trust me son, if I could go over there and kill the Kaiser myself, I would."

Leroy was relieved to hear that Ella was not the enemy. He relaxed his eyes and lowered his shoulders, but he had one more question. "Do you think they'll come over here to fight us like they are in France?"

Ella sat silently for a moment with her hands firmly cupped on her lap. She understood the hatred in Leroy's words and knew he spoke them out of fear. Before responding to Leroy's question, she took a slow, deep breath. "No, my dear boy. They would never be foolish enough to attack us here, because they know they would never win. I assure you that if they did come here, I would kill every last German myself to keep you and Ruby safe."

Suddenly Leroy regretted his earlier comments about killing all Germans, realizing that would have included Ella. "Um—Ella, I'm sorry for what I said before. I didn't mean anything by it."

Ella's face softened. "That's quite all right, Leroy. I enjoyed our conversation tonight. Now you best hurry up and eat some of that great food your sister prepared before it gets too cold."

With a tip of his baseball hat toward Ella, Leroy ran off to the kitchen.

To Ruby's amazement her little brother never questioned Ella's attire that evening. Even after several more visits from Ella, Leroy seemed more interested in talking with her about the war rushing through Europe than what she was wearing.

NINETEEN

December 31, 1914

It had been snowing all night, the first heavy snow of the winter. Ruby got dressed and went downstairs to see the transformation that had occurred as they slept. When she stepped onto the front porch, there was an eerie silence. The landscape was void of sound: no wind, birds, or cows. Even Leroy's trusted dog, Foxy, who would usually come to greet her when the front door was opened, was nowhere in sight. As it started to snow again, she could see how big and heavy with moisture the flakes were, and could almost hear them as they landed in the soft pillows of white that had formed around the house.

There were no outside chores to be done today, she thought with a smile. Once the cows were milked and fed, the day belonged to her and Ella. Her father had been expected home that afternoon, but she knew there would be no way for him to get through the heavy snow on the roads, possibly for days. There would also be no way for her houseguests to leave in the near future, either.

Ella and Olga had come to visit the sisters for New Year's. They had all planned on going to Cora's house that evening to ring in the new year. However, the heavy snow made going anywhere impossible. With that thought, Ruby ran upstairs to tell Ella.

Ella was still asleep, but Ruby couldn't wait to share the news. She jumped on the bed and cried, "Guess what, Ella?"

Ella was startled, but kept her eyes closed. "Ruby, unless your father is driving up to the house right now, I'm still asleep."

"No, Ella, it's wonderful outside! You've got to wake up and see it."

"Ruby, the last time I was outside it looked like it was going to rain. So how can it be wonderful?" Ella asked, still unwilling to open her eyes.

"It's snowing now, and it's been snowing all night. There's no way for Papa to come home, and there's no way for you to leave. At least any time soon."

There was still no response from Ella.

Ruby was disappointed that Ella wasn't reacting to her exciting news and appeared to have fallen back to sleep. Ruby bounced back to her side of the bed. "Alright, then. You just go ahead and sleep all day if you want. That's just fine with me." Ruby sat there for a moment with her arms crossed.

All of a sudden, Ella grabbed Ruby from behind and started tickling her. "So, Pete, is that your big news for the morning?" she asked.

Ruby was laughing so hard she could barely answer Ella's question. "Yes, yes, that's my big news for the day. Now stop tickling me before we wake up everyone in the house."

The request came too late. Ruby could hear someone in the kitchen putting wood in the stove. "Now see what you've done. Someone is up already."

"Me? You're the one who wanted to share with the world that it's snowing outside. I was perfectly happy sleeping next to you."

Ruby got out of bed and went downstairs, where she was surprised to see her brother. "Leroy, what are you doing in the kitchen?"

"I'm hungry, and the way you gals all sleep a fella could starve to death before you get around to making breakfast."

Ruby knew her little brother was feeling lonely, and she felt bad that she hadn't paid much attention to him in the last few months. Since meeting Ella, her life had been centered around her own feelings of happiness, and focused on when she and Ella would see each other again.

"Leroy, how about I make us breakfast, and after the dishes are done we can all do something together?"

Ruby saw his face light up as he asked, "Like what? It's snowing outside."

Ruby thought for a moment. "How about if we all get dressed up for New Year's and you take some pictures?"

She knew Leroy always loved taking photos, and it didn't matter much to him if it was sunny outside or not. "Really? Okay, hurry up and make breakfast so I can go get the camera cleaned up and ready to go."

Ruby was pleased to see Leroy just as happy as she was. However, she wasn't sure how happy the girls were going to be when she told them they needed to get dressed up for photos in the snow.

TWENTY

I remember my Grandma Ruby vividly. She was a petite woman with a gravelly voice, like heavy smokers have, though I'd never known her to smoke. She didn't have a lot to say, and it always seemed like she was missing something, or like something had been taken away from her. I guess, to an extent, something was.

Always insisting on looking her best, she would wear colorful floral dresses and matching shoes with a slight heel. Her favorite color was purple. When my mom and I would go shopping for her birthday or Christmas presents, Mom would usually pick out a nice purple outfit with all the necessary accessories.

One year for Christmas, Mom bought Grandma a lightweight, purple knitted sweater. Nothing fancy, just something to keep her arms warm because she always told us how cold she was. She loved that little sweater, and wore it so often the sleeves started to unravel at the cuffs. When Grandma could no longer repair it, she would simply roll up the sleeves to hide the loose threads. Even in the hot, humid St. Louis summers, she insisted on wearing it over her lightweight dresses. Mom bought other pullovers for her to wear, but whenever we saw Grandma she would be wearing that same tattered purple sweater.

I was with my mom in Missouri when she was going through her mother's belongings after the funeral. I remember seeing that sweater hanging in the closet and watching my mother reach for it. She smiled, thinking about how much her mother loved wearing it. Then she took it off the hanger and lifted the sweater to her face to smell her mother one last time, before putting it in a box marked for Goodwill. My mom never threw anything away; she thought someone could repair the sleeves, but I'm sure that never happened.

Grandma loved taking pictures, and would carry a camera with her wherever she went. One of the first cameras I recall her having was a little boxy Kodak—the kind of camera you would look through the top of and the picture would magically appear right-side-up in the viewfinder. When I was a kid, I was fascinated by it and spent hours trying to figure out how it worked, not knowing at the time that it was a system of mirrors which transferred the image to the top of the camera.

One of my fondest memories of Grandma was her homemade doughnuts. To this day, I still remember how delicious those doughnuts were, coming right out of the bubbling hot oil. The worst part was waiting for them to cool off enough to safely eat one without burning my mouth. She made up a game of cooling them off by seeing who could blow the hardest on the newly-fried dough. Of course, then she would tell me I'd won and hand me a doughnut as a prize.

Grandma lived in an apartment in St. Louis in the late sixties. I remember that whenever my mom and I would visit her, we always had to bring her a case of Coors beer. Grandma loved her Coors, but it wasn't sold in 'Budweiser Country' Missouri at that time. So, my mom would pack up a case of beer and have it shipped with us on the airplane all the way from Los Angeles. Grandma Ruby said it helped thicken her blood for the cold winters.

Grandma Ruby also suffered with dementia in her later years, and eventually Mom had her placed in a nursing home in Missouri. I hated going there. It smelled like urine, and it seemed like people were just lying there waiting to die. One time while we were there I noticed that some of the patients had been tied to their wheelchairs, and I remember asking my mom why. She explained that it was 'for their own good' because some of them might fall out and get hurt. It was horribly depressing, and my grandma would always beg us to take her home. Mom wanted to, but she was working full-time in Los Angeles. She knew her mother needed around-the-clock attention and couldn't afford the more costly facilities in California.

Before leaving the nursing home on one of our last visits, Mom told me to wait in the car while she talked to the nurse at the front desk. I wasn't sure what she talked with them about, but I could tell she had been crying when she returned to the car. I pretended not to notice; I figured it was because of the poor conditions her mother was living in, and how helpless she felt to change things.

Mom would often get phone calls from the nursing home threatening to kick Grandma out because she was untying the other patients from their wheelchairs, which was causing them to fall to the floor. Mom would immediately phone Grandma to reason with her. "Why in the world would you do such a thing, Mother? Don't you understand that people could get hurt?"

Grandma's standard response was, "Oh, I don't know, dear. I suppose I did it because they asked me to. They said they just wanted to be free to move around."

I know it's not funny, but I must admit at the time we did laugh about that. However, I now have a better understanding of why she would say and do such a thing. She wanted them freed from the bonds that tied them. Free to move around without the restrictions others placed on them.

I watched my mom prepare the boxes of Grandma's belongings after she passed, much like I did years later when she passed away on April 21, 2013. It felt odd, that all I had after my mother passed was only a few boxes to remember her by. Or maybe that's just how it's supposed to be. We spend so much of our lives collecting things, but in the end, after it's all been sold or given away, it only amounts to a few simple boxes.

Grandma Ruby 1969   *Top Grandma Ruby 1959*

Me and Grandma Ruby in Hawaii 1971

DON'T YOU DARE

TWENTY-ONE

March 12, 1915

Ella caught the No. 6 train to Amherst after teaching her last class Friday afternoon. She hated taking the train, preferring to drive her own car, especially when going to Cora's. When driving she could wear her gentleman's suit, hat, and gloves, without anyone suspecting she was anything other than a gentleman driver. However, in March there was too much snow on the narrow Wisconsin roads, making driving hazardous. Still, she had to see Ruby.

Ella managed to get a seat next to the window and began to relax as she felt the train slowly pull away from the station. As she listened to the sound of the wheels turning on the tracks and felt the swaying motion of the train, her eyes started getting heavy. She quickly sat up in her chair to avoid the temptation of falling asleep, and started watching the landscape pass as she moved ever closer to her beloved. Occasionally, she would wipe the moisture from the inside of the windows with the handkerchief she kept tucked inside her sleeve. She made a circle just large enough to see the farms and old barns going by. Being familiar with the area, she knew it would be another hour before the train would arrive.

Gazing out the window, she thought about the last time she was in Amherst. She remembered waking up next to Ruby that New Year's Eve morning and how excited Ruby was to tell her about the snow outside.

Ruby's laughter as she tickled her, and how they dressed up in their best clothes just to go outside in the snow so Leroy could take a picture. She smiled to herself, thinking about all they had shared in those five days, and felt her heart start to race.

Ella told herself to slow down and not get carried away with such emotion.

It wasn't that long ago that Ella was to start her new profession as a teacher, and a new life with Alice. Alice was a librarian she'd met in college, and they'd planned to move to Portland, Oregon after Ella graduated. Ella had been to Portland before to visit friends and family, and had already made arrangements for her and Alice to stay with some of them until the two of them found jobs. There they could both earn a good living and not worry about the interference of Alice's family. However, once Alice's parents found out about her leaving town with Ella, they quickly became involved and had her placed in a psychiatric hospital until she agreed to marry the nephew of one of her father's coworkers.

Alice had broken her heart badly, and she wasn't yet convinced that Ruby wouldn't do the same. Ella still yearned for the West Coast, and dreamt of the day she would move there with the woman she loved. There they would walk on the beach together, and she would smell the sweet, salty air of the Pacific Ocean once again. Most of all, she desired a love that no one could take away from her.

Ella began to recognize the houses just outside of Amherst, and she felt the momentum of the train begin to slow. Then came the sound of the brakes hissing and screeching as the conductor slowed the powerful steam engine. In a few moments the train would pull into the station. She thought to herself, *Why in the world would Cora have a sleigh ride in the middle of March? Only she would think of such a crazy thing.*

During the winter months, everyone was starting to get cabin fever. So, Cora decided to hold an event in the snow by hosting a sleigh ride for about twenty-five of the ladies. She sent word that they were all to meet at

2:30 p.m. in front of the Central Hotel, which was located in the middle of town. Cora considered that the horse-drawn sleighs lined up on Main Street would be quite a spectacle, and informed the chums not to wear their gentlemen's clothing because all the people in town would be looking at them. She didn't want to draw too much unwanted attention.

Once the train stopped, Ella cleared the window one last time, hoping to see Ruby standing on the platform. As she placed the handkerchief back in her sleeve she glanced down to straighten her dress. She was wearing a long black dress that came down just above her ankles, and an ivory-and-black tailored wool coat with large white buttons on the front. Ella looked very much like a teacher, with her hair pulled up into a high, tight bun. She wasn't at all comfortable, but she knew it had to be done if she wanted to see Ruby.

Ruby arrived at the station just before the train pulled in, not wanting to miss the feeling of the warm steam on her face. She closed her eyes for a moment to smell the hot oil from the huge locomotive engine as it slowly made its way past her to the passenger platform. Ruby loved everything about going to the train station. She watched the giant turning wheels come to a stop and waited for the passengers to make their way off. Normally she would watch the people arriving and make up stories in her head about where they might be traveling to or from, but this time she was only looking for one person.

In the last few months, Ruby and Ella had managed to talk to each other only a couple of times on the phone. The general store in Lime Lake had a phone, but it was a party line shared by neighbors. When Ruby was able to get an open line to Ella, they both knew their conversation was likely listened to—sometimes by accident, but mostly as a form of entertainment or a way of spreading town gossip. Mindful of this, their conversations were never romantic toward each other. Mail delivery was the fastest and most effective form of communication; however, it was not the safest. Ruby would use the return name of Pete Peterson on envelopes addressed to Ella, and Ella used Mr. O'Brien on letters addressed to Ruby. That way, if someone opened their letters, they would appear to be written between a man and woman.

Ruby used Ella's given name when they were alone, but Ella preferred the name of Mr. O'Brien when dressed as a gent at parties or for photos.

Ruby stood next to the train as it arrived, looking for Ella everywhere. She knew she'd be wearing a dress, as Cora had requested. Since Ruby had never seen her in a dress before, she was afraid she might not be able to spot her right away.

When the steam cleared, she saw Ella standing next to the train and ran over to give her a hug and a kiss on the cheek. Ella looked uncomfortable, and seemed annoyed by having to wear such attire. "I don't know why Cora insisted that we all had to wear our dresses. I would be much warmer and happier wearing my suit and hat."

"Come on, Ella, you look beautiful. It'll be a lot of fun. I saw some of the gals are already at the hotel where the sleighs are. Besides, you will always be Mr. O'Brien to me," Ruby said with a smile. Keeping hold of Ella's waist, she pulled her and her suitcase in the direction of the hotel.

As they made their way to the hotel, Ella saw Van and Drake standing out front. The three of them all had the same miserable looks on their faces: the kind of look kids have when their mothers dress them up for Sunday church. Ruby and the other ladies did their best to cheer up the chums, but until they got into their gentlemen's attire there would be no pleasing them.

Soon Cora arrived with blankets and started loading up the ladies into sleighs. The two-hour ride took them to Nelsonville and the surrounding area. The best part of the ride for Ella and Ruby was sharing a blanket together. Their faces were flushed from the cold wind, as well as from holding hands underneath the heavy wool blanket. As Ella stroked the top of Ruby's hand with her thumb, she knew there was no other place she'd rather be.

The sun was setting and the temperature was beginning to drop, but there was plenty of warmth underneath the blanket. Even Ella, who'd been convinced that a good time would not be had, was now hoping the ride would continue just a little while longer.

The horse-drawn sleighs landed at Cora's home, where all the girls were greeted with hot cocoa and a hearty supper. Before the chums could even think about food, they rushed upstairs to change out of their dresses and into their suits and ties. Ella, Van, Drake, and a few of the other chums returned to the dinning room with huge expressions of relief.

The remainder of the evening was grand. Cora's home was a bundle of pent-up energy releasing itself from the darkness of the cold weather. After dinner they all sat in the parlor, listening to live music played by Ralph Mathieson.

Ralph was a local bandleader and pianist who was a frequent guest at the usually 'ladies only' parties. Ralph loved going to Cora's because he, too, could put on his best dress for the evening. Before the other ladies and chums arrived, one of the gals would sit him down and make sure his makeup was done to perfection. He loved watching his transformation in the mirror as the makeup was applied. Each step of the process took him closer to his true self.

The ladies referred to Ralph as their 'tickled fellow.' They didn't mind a man being there because they considered him to be one of the girls. When he grew tired of playing piano or felt like dancing, the Victor Victrola would start playing. As laughter filled the room, each of the ladies and chums would take turns dancing with Ralph. The sound of laughter was so loud that sometimes the music couldn't be heard over it, but that didn't stop them. They would keep dancing and spinning in the middle of the room, spinning so fast that some of the ladies had to sit down for fear of falling. It was a beautiful sight to see. Women dressed as men, dancing with a man dressed as a woman. A beautiful sight indeed...

Gazette (Stevens Point, Wisconsin)
March 10, 1915

On Monday afternoon of last week Miss Cora Turner was the hostess of a sleighride party. About 36 ladies met at the Central Hotel, where rigs were provided. Upon their return they were taken to the home of Miss Turner; where a substantial hot lunch was served.

TWENTY-TWO

April 11, 2014

After searching the 1910 Portage County map at the local library, I found where I needed to go next: I had located the Peterson family farm, where my grandmother lived a hundred years ago. The name of the road had changed over the years, but because I had driven around so much in the last few days, I knew exactly where to find it.

After a quick fifteen-minute drive from where I was staying, I turned left onto Lime Lake Road, spotted the sign marked 'Private Road-No Outlet,' and kept driving anyway. It was a narrow one-lane gravel road with no other houses in sight. Driving about a half a mile down the road, I could feel my skin tingling and my heart beating faster as I recognized the rolling hillsides that were in the background of so many of my grandmother's photos. There was a bend in the road around the hillside, and then I saw it: the house, the red barn, the huge boulders in the front pasture. Even the old metal windmill was still standing.

The road ended as it circled around the house. I parked the car and sat there for a moment to regain my composure. I knew someone was living there, because everything was well-maintained. The main house looked like it had been updated, but it was still recognizable from the photos I had. The barn, on the other hand, was a bit dilapidated. The red paint was cracking and most of the windows were broken. Still, it looked beautifully familiar to me.

I glanced back at the house; I could tell someone was peeking through the curtains at me. I'm sure not many visitors came out this way unless they were selling something. I just hoped whoever was watching me didn't feel the need to greet me with a shotgun.

Grabbing a binder with some of the old farm photos I'd brought with me, I started walking toward the house. My plan was to show whoever lived there the photos and explain why I was there as quickly as possible. I was also hoping they would be willing to let me walk around the property and take some pictures.

There was no need for me to knock on the door, because I heard it creak open a little as soon as I walked up. It was cracked just enough that I could see an old woman standing in the doorway. I guessed she was in her late eighties or early nineties. She was careful not to open the door all the way as I introduced myself and told her right away why I was there. I'm sure I was talking very fast, because I was afraid she would think I was selling something and close the door on me.

I took out my binder of photos to show her what her house and barn looked like in the early 1900s. As I was doing this, I could see her starting to smile. Once she knew I was not a threat or selling anything, she stepped out of the house to greet me. "My name is Dorothy, but I'm afraid I don't know who the Petersons are."

As Dorothy left the safety of her house, I couldn't help noticing how much she reminded me of my own mother, who had passed away only twelve months before. She had the same kind, welcoming smile, and a sparkle in her eyes that made me miss my mother even more.

We talked for a few minutes. She shared with me that she had raised her three sons there and they had made some improvements to the original house over the years. The basketball hoop next to an old shed had clearly seen its share of afternoon games with her boys.

It was cold outside, and I could tell she was eager to get back inside where it was warm. Feeling protective, because she reminded me so much of my mom, I urged her to go inside before she caught a cold. Before she left, I asked Dorothy if it was okay if I walked around and took some photos of her property, which she graciously agreed to.

As she closed the door, I turned around and took a few steps. There I was, standing at the 'Home Sweet Home' of the Peterson family, between the house and the old red barn. I felt the brisk wind on my face. It had rained the night before, and I could smell the sweet wet earth underneath my feet. There were no cows, horses, or even a dog on the property, but it still looked and felt much like the old family farm.

I started wandering, thinking how lucky Dorothy's sons had been to grow up on such beautiful land. It was a little sad to learn the Peterson name had vanished from the property, but I was happy to think about all the family memories that had occurred here just the same.

I walked around the house, taking photos as I went. I could tell Dorothy was still keeping an eye on me from the warmth of her home, but I didn't mind.

It was silent, except for the sound of the wind blowing some of the last remaining dried leaves on the trees, and the crunching of gravel under my feet as I walked toward the front of the house. Overlooking the pastures, which had once been potato fields, I made out the two large boulders by the old wooden fence. I looked at the picture in my binder to confirm. Yes—these were the same boulders that were in some of my grandmother's photos. I just stood there staring at them, imagining how much fun the ladies and chums had had taking photos of each other in that very same spot so long ago. The photos taken there were entitled: 'All dressed up and no place to go,' 'All push no pull,' and 'Don't You Dare.' I could hear my grandmother and the gals laughing in joy, with the same playfulness shown in the pictures.

I kept walking around the house to examine the old red barn. There was still a little winter snow on the northern side of the barn, which had yet to see the direct sunlight of the changing season. I once again matched up the photos of the old farm. Even though the paint and windows had seen better days, the structure seemed just as solid as it was one hundred years ago. The thought of exploring inside the barn did cross my mind, but I didn't want to push my luck with Dorothy. Though, with the stories that old barn could tell, I would have loved to have gone inside.

Behind the house, next to the barn, was a clothesline that was still being used by Dorothy. Beyond that I could see what looked to be a little shrine of sorts. It seemed religious in nature, with a small statue of what I thought was Mother Mary. It was a beautiful little area, and seemed to be about the same location where Ruby and Ella's wedding photos would have been taken. I peered back at the house and saw Dorothy was keeping a watchful eye on me from her window. I was drawn to the area where the statue was and wanted to walk toward it, but instead I started to head back to the house.

As if on cue, the door magically opened again. I thanked Dorothy for letting me walk around, and handed her one of the photos of her property from one hundred years ago. It felt like the right thing to do. I wanted to give her something; or maybe the photo just needed to stay where it came from. She seemed very pleased, and asked me again what my great-grandfather's name was. "Peter Peterson," I responded, and so she wouldn't forget I wrote my grandfather's name on the side of the photo and handed it back. She thanked me and gave me a warm smile goodbye.

It was hard walking away from the old Peterson home, but I wanted to be respectful of Dorothy and her family by not overstaying my welcome. Before getting into my car, I stopped and looked up at the two broken windows at the very top of the weathered red barn one more time. I smiled to myself, thinking about my ancestors and the events that occurred there. As I slowly drove away, I couldn't help noticing how energized I felt, and how surreal my adventure of finding out more about my grandmother had become. I was in no hurry to return to the main highway, as I committed every boulder and tree to memory.

All dressed up and no place to go.
Ruby (second from the right)

Don't you Dare
Ruby on the right

Ruby on the right
All Pull and no push March
27, 1916

April 11, 2014

TWENTY-THREE

June 6, 1915

With spring flowers in full bloom, June has always been the most popular time of year for young lovers to schedule marriage. Wedding ceremonies that had been planned well in advance now gave rise to parties with friends, and family gatherings to celebrate the impending nuptials of the many brides and grooms.

Linen parties and showers were given for the bride as a way to provide her with all the necessary items to start a proper new home. Wicker baskets were filled with items such as linen tablecloths, cloth napkins, and placemats. Even laundry detergents and cotton softener would be decorated with colorful ribbons and bows. Ladies would wear their best party or tea dresses, wide-brimmed hats adorned with feathers, and flowers attached with hatpins.

Schools were closed for spring break, and Ella was in town attending such a party for one of the ladies in the group at Cora's home. However, this was not the typical jovial linen party. There was no excitement about the upcoming wedding from the bride-to-be. Nor was there any desire from the unwed women at the party to be in her place. It was a going-away party, of sorts: one last bittersweet hurrah with the ladies and chums, the friends and hidden lovers, before being married to a young man and leaving for a life most of them knew little about.

Cora did her best to supply a party full of fun and games for the gals, but the heaviness of the impending wedding hung in the room like a water-soaked wool sweater. Over the years, Cora had held dozens of these parties, for the women who would come and go. She'd stopped asking herself, "How will this one adjust to her new life?" a long time ago. She'd become accustomed to the inevitable goodbyes of an uncertain fate.

In one of the last letters my Grandma Ruby wrote, she compared getting married to "Going to war and fighting a battle. A battle for her life." This sentiment, I'm sure, was shared with the other ladies in the group.

Women attending these linen parties tried to rally their courage and put on a strong front for each other. Crying was not allowed. It was meant as a show of unity and support for each other, in a time when there were no other options. At the party, they would all be thinking the same thing: "Will I be next?"

"Come on, Pete, go with me to the party," Ella begged Ruby as she was getting dressed at the Peterson home.

"No, Ella, I will not go to another one of those horribly depressing parties. Why do they insist on calling it a party, anyway? No one is happy to be there. We just stand around the room looking at each other, trying to guess who will be the next victim. No, I tell you. I will not go."

Ella knew how stubborn Ruby could be, and that there would be no way of changing her mind. "All right then. Have it your way, Pete," she said, struggling with her tie.

Ruby reached from behind Ella to help her with the tie and asked, "What do you think will happen to me if I'm required to get married?"

Her stomach cringed at the thought. "I suppose that's up to you, Pete. How can I possibly answer that question for you? I only know that I will never marry a man. Not now—not ever." Ella's answer was adamant.

Ruby shot back, "That's so easy for you to say and do. You have a teaching career and can support yourself. I don't. Your parents don't care what you do or how you live your life. You don't have to worry about disappointing anyone, because you only have yourself to think about."

Ruby knew her words were hurtful, but it was too late to take them back. Ella had never seen Ruby so angry. She reached for Ruby's hand. "I am sorry, Pete, I didn't mean to upset you. I know it's difficult for you and the other girls, but you need to start thinking what you'll do when that time comes."

"That's just it, Ella—I don't know what I will do. I suppose I'll delay it as long as I can, but how will I bear leaving you and our pals?"

"Why should you?" Ella asked.

"What do you mean?" Ruby responded sharply.

Ella turned to Ruby. "Why don't you come with me to Portland, on the West Coast, in Oregon? You would love it, Pete. People are so friendly there; nothing like the people here. They're much more open-minded. I've already been offered a teaching job at Jefferson High School, and with my earnings I could support us both. I can buy us a house on the most beautiful piece of land you will ever see. One side of the house will overlook the mountains, and the other side the Pacific Ocean. It rains a lot, but hardly ever snows. Oh my, wait till you see the sunsets there. Pete, you would..."

Ruby yelled, "Ella, please stop! Just stop. This is too much for me to think about right now. How could I just leave my family? I would never see my brothers or sisters again. What would happen to my father? He needs me, you know."

Ella looked down and realized her biggest fear: Ruby was not yet ready to commit fully to her. "My darling, I'm not asking you to make that decision for yourself now. However, you must certainly realize your father will expect marriage of you in the near future? I'm simply suggesting you consider what I've offered, and the life we could have together. I promise never to speak of it again."

Deep down, Ruby knew Ella was right, but the thought of that day petrified her. She preferred to pretend it would never happen. However, she agreed to Ella's request to consider moving to Portland as Ella dressed for the 'linen party.' Still upset, Ruby remained sitting in her mother's armchair next to the window, deep in thought.

Ella swiped the lint from her suit jacket one last time and looked in Ruby's direction. She knew it would be pointless arguing with her any longer, but there was one last thing she had to say before leaving. As she walked toward the front door, Ella stopped, leaned down and lightly kissed Ruby's forehead. "I love you, Ruby Peterson," she whispered.

Ruby watched Ella put on her driving gloves as she walked toward her car, clearly disappointed about leaving alone to the party. Ruby was so lost in her thoughts that she hadn't paid attention to what Ella just told her. She sat there a few moments longer before realization struck her. *Did Ella tell me she loved me?*

Ruby jumped out of the chair and ran through the kitchen to catch Ella before she left. She looked outside the window before opening the back door and saw that it was too late. Ella had already left the driveway and was well on her way to Cora's house. Ruby stood looking out the window for a few more minutes, hoping she would turn the car around and come back home to her.

After a while, Ruby returned to the comfort of her mother's chair and continued gazing out the window, praying Ella would sense her desires and return home sooner rather than later. Looking down at the chair, she saw that the fabric had started to fade from the direct sunlight, and some of the stitching had come undone around the corner. It had been three short years since her mother passed, and so much had happened. She knew if her mother were there she'd be able to repair her life as well as the fabric on her favorite chair.

She wished she could talk to her mother one last time. She closed her eyes and held on to the arms of the chair, pretending she was holding her mother's hands. "Mama, am I crazy? Am I ever going to find happiness in this life? What shall I do? I don't want to disappoint Papa, but I'm afraid I might."

Ruby prayed to hear the comfort of her mother's voice telling her, "Everything will be fine," but all she heard was the bustle of the blossoming tree limbs rubbing against the side of the house in the wind. She looked out the window again; still no Ella.

The window overlooked the front pasture, where the newly planted potatoes were just starting to sprout. *Not much to be done until they grow a little higher*, she thought. Alone with her thoughts, Ruby spent the next few hours gazing out the window, looking for answers to questions so few people understood.

When Ella returned from the party, she found Ruby asleep in the very same chair she was in when she left, curled up to keep her legs warm. Ella wondered if she'd been there all that time. She knelt quietly in front of Ruby and watched her sleep for a moment, then gently woke her by kissing her hand.

Ruby was so tired, yet relived to see Ella. She held out her arms to welcome her home and said, "I love you, too."

TWENTY-FOUR

June 7, 1915

The next morning Ruby woke up to Ella holding her tightly; so tightly she could feel Ella's heart beating inside her own. The sun had not yet warmed the night air, and they were wrapped in a cocoon of blankets. As she lay there in Ella's arms listening to her breathe, she wished they could stay that way forever. Ella's embrace gave her comfort as she glanced at the family photos hanging on her bedroom wall.

Ruby realized that it was the first time she ever envisioned spending the rest of her life with someone. She started dreaming of the beautiful home Ella had mentioned, overlooking the Pacific Ocean surrounded by mountains. At last a vision of what she wanted seemed so incredibly clear. She stayed there for a few more minutes, enjoying an absolute contentment and blissfulness she had never felt before.

Soon Ruby's eyes welled up with tears, which ran quietly down her face. *Why now?* she thought. *How could life be so cruel as to curse me with such impossible visions? What have I done that God would punish me this way?*

Ruby felt her world spinning to the point that she could no longer breathe, and jumped out of bed.

Ella was startled as Ruby pulled away from her embrace. Seeing the fear in Ruby's eyes, she started to panic. "Is your father home?" she asked, quickly untangling herself from the blankets before leaping to the floor and grabbing her clothes.

Ruby said nothing. Ella was still trying to focus. She ran to the bedroom window, expecting to see Mr. Peterson's car in the driveway, but saw nothing.

"Pete, what is so horribly wrong? Please tell me!"

Ruby sat on the end of her bed with tears running down her face. Ella could tell there was no emergency outside, but a personal one in front of her that was perhaps more important. She sat next to Ruby. They stayed there in silence for a moment, both of them trying to catch their breath.

Ella took one last deep breath and reached for Ruby's hand. "My love, what upset you so? Have I done something wrong?"

Ruby was still trying to think of what to say when Ella gently kissed her cheek. "Please Ruby, talk to me. I must know so I can make sure that it never happens again. I never want to see you so upset."

How Ruby wished Ella understood without her having to speak. "It's just a foolish vision of us living together as one, living in a beautiful home. We'd still have to hide our love from others. The only future we could possibly share is just this week, this day, this moment of time, and no more. Or could we?" Ruby stood up. "If you were a gent, would you ask me to marry you?"

Ella fumbled to compose herself. "My lovely Ruby, I adore and love you. I would be honored if you could be my wife." As soon as Ella said that, she felt an ache run though her; she knew marriage to the one she loved would never be.

Ruby felt the heaviness in the room, but she was determined that something could and should be done about it. "Well then, I think you should propose marriage to me."

Ella wasn't sure she'd heard Ruby correctly. "Did you just say you want me to propose to you?"

"No, I said I think you should propose to me. That is, if you really do love me and want to share a life together? Or were you just telling me those things for no reason at all?"

Ella was used to Ruby's assertiveness, but still this request surprised her. Even Ruby was a little surprised after she said it; such things were never heard of. However, she wasn't one to say things she didn't mean.

"Yes, that's exactly what I meant, Ella. I want to be your wife."

Ella stumbled over her words. "Ruby Peterson, you know that no church, let alone minister or reverend in this world, will ever allow such a thing. In fact, we might get arrested or thrown into the loony bin for even suggesting such a crazy thing."

Of course Ruby knew Ella was right, but she insisted, "How about if we have our wedding here, out back by the trees next to the garden? It's a beautiful little spot. Ada and Sara will be in town tomorrow. My sister can be my maid of honor, and I'm sure Sara would be willing to be your best man. If she didn't bring a suit you can lend her one of yours. I'm sure Leroy would be more than happy to be the photographer."

By now Ella was looking at Ruby as though she had totally lost her mind. "Pete, slow down. Do you know what you are asking us to do? What if someone finds out—and I mean anyone, even some of our pals? If word gets out about such a thing, what would happen to us?"

"Ella, no one will find out. Only the five of us will ever know we are married."

Still trying to understand why Ruby wanted to do such a dangerous thing, Ella stopped to consider what a wedding ceremony would mean for them both. "Do you mean to move with me to Portland, Pete? Is that what you're trying to tell me? With this wedding ceremony, would you be willing to leave this place and your family behind?"

Ruby smiled at Ella. "Well, Mr. O'Brien, if I am your wife then I must go where you go."

Ella shot up from where she had been sitting and walked toward the window to consider Ruby's words. She waited for the cool breeze to dry the sweat on her forehead before turning around to face Ruby. Her face was without emotion as she walked to Ruby. As she stood face to face with her, Ella's eyes began to well with tears. She reached for Ruby's hands and knelt on both knees. "Ruby Sarah Peterson, would you do me the great honor of becoming my wife?"

TWENTY-FIVE

June 8, 1915

Ruby had been awake since the sun crested the hillside, and was lying in bed listening to the sound of songbirds outside her window. She watched the tapestry curtains billowing in the light breeze coming through her open window on what would surely be a memorable day. In her room alone, Ruby looked once again at the photos of her family and friends hanging on the walls. She tried to imagine what it would be like to live somewhere other than the only place she had always known as home. She wondered what it would it be like looking at different-colored wallpaper, put up by a stranger's hands and not her father's. She'd spent hours imagining what would become of her someday. Now it seemed some of her questions would soon be answered.

Ella slept downstairs in a room that had belonged to Ruby's older brother, Elmer, who had moved away from home long ago. Ruby insisted they were not to see each other until the appropriate time of their wedding. When Ruby heard a car approaching the house, she hoped it was Ada and Sara driving in from Steven's Point. She looked out her bedroom window. "They're here!" Ruby shouted out so Ella could hear as she put on her robe and headed downstairs to give Ada and Sara the news.

Sara Wilson was a music teacher in town. She and Ada were returning from another teachers' conference they had attended in Stevens Point.

Sara considered herself very much a lady and enjoyed the highest fashion available at that time; however, she would don gentlemen's clothing from time to time as well.

Ruby ran out to the car to greet them. "I'm so happy you're here, I have some exciting news for you both."

Sara looked at Ada and raised her eyebrows as if to ask silently, 'What is your sister up to now?'

Ada knew she had to ask, but she was never sure what to expect from her younger sister. With her eyes closed, she said, "Okay, Ruby what's your exciting news today?"

"We're getting married," Ruby stated proudly.

Ada's eyes shot open. "What are you talking about, Ruby? Who is getting married?"

Ruby was still grinning from ear to ear. "Ella and me. We're getting married, and you both are invited. Well, actually you are both going to be in the wedding. Ada, you'll be my maid of honor, and Sara will be Ella's best man, or chum if you prefer. Ella has an extra suit you can wear if you didn't bring yours."

Still in the car, Ada and Sara sat motionless, stunned speechless by Ruby's wedding arrangements. Sara finally looked at Ada and said, "You know, your sister is a crazy one. Does she know she's crazy?"

Ada looked at Ruby. "Sara is right. You are crazy. You can't get married to Ella, or any woman for that matter. Ruby Peterson, have you lost your mind?"

"No, I have not lost my mind. We're not going to a church, and there won't be a reverend here. We'll all get dressed up, and Ella and I will exchange vows and take some photographs. It doesn't seem very difficult to me, and we'll have a grand party afterwards. Are you two going to join us on this glorious day or not?"

Ruby was waiting for a response with her hands perched on her hips. Ada noticed that Ella was nowhere to be found. "Where is Ella? I don't even see her. Does she know about this ludicrous idea of yours?"

"Of course she does. I had her sleep in Elmer's old room. I don't want her to see me until I have my wedding dress on. It's bad luck, you know."

Ada shook her head in disbelief. "I think you're both crazy. What if someone from town finds out about this wedding of yours? How could we possibly explain it to Papa? His business could be ruined, you know, and we could all be run out of town for doing such a thing. Ruby, you must be careful. You could get hurt or put away. We all could."

Ada looked at Sara and then back to Ruby. She could tell that Ruby was unwavering in her desire to marry Ella.

"Well then, as long as you know what you're getting yourself—and us—into. I'd better go talk to your groom-to-be."

Ruby jumped up and down. "Sister, does that mean you and Sara will do this for us?"

Ada glanced over to Sara. "What do you think about all of this?"

Sara thought for a moment. "I think you are all crazy to do such a thing, and I must be just as crazy too. I have a suit with me, but I didn't bring a hat for photos. Lord help us all if anyone finds out about this."

All this time Ella had been waiting in Elmer's room, trying to hear what the girls out front were saying. She knew their plan for a wedding was daring and risky, for many reasons. She was concerned that Ruby's sister might not approve of or allow such a thing. Still, all she could think about was Ruby standing by her side in a wedding dress.

Ella had always dreamt about what it would be like to walk down the aisle toward her beloved. She imagined being dressed in her best gentleman's garments and standing next to the woman she loved; then looking into the eyes of her beautiful bride and saying the two words that mattered the most. There was a fire deep inside her that needed to say the simple words, 'I do' to the woman she loved.

"What could be taking them so long?" she thought.

Ella was growing impatient, and her stomach was grumbling from lack of food. She slowly opened the squeaky bedroom door, with the plan of sneaking some food from the kitchen and possibly overhearing what was being said outside. Then she heard Ruby, Ada, and Sara coming into the house. She quickly stepped back into the room and closed the door behind her.

Ada knocked on Elmer's bedroom door. "Ella, are you still in there? It's not too late for you to get out of this if you haven't already escaped out the bedroom window."

"Nope, I'm still here," Ella responded, but she was still unsure how Ada and Sara were taking the news.

Ada stood outside the door and asked, "Ella, do you really want to go through with this crazy wedding idea my sister told me about?"

The room that Ella had been waiting in suddenly seemed much smaller. Beads of sweat began forming on her top lip. "Yes, ma'am, very much." Ella wanted to say more, but she could feel her throat tightening up.

Ada could hear how nervous Ella was. "I suppose if you're going to be my brother-in-law I should go fix you a good breakfast for your big day."

Ella was so relieved by Ada's response. "Oh, Ada. Thank you so much! That is, thank you for being a part of our wedding. Also, thank you for making breakfast. I'm starving in here. Is Ruby outside the door? Can I come out now?"

Ruby started laughing. "Mr. O'Brien, you stay in there. Sara will bring you your breakfast while I start getting ready. After you both eat, you need to start getting dressed. Ada and I will be getting ready upstairs. You two must stay down here. No peeking."

TWENTY-SIX

There was no fear, no second thoughts about what might happen if they were caught. There would be no need to hide their love for each other. Ruby was ready to commit, and Ella's dream of standing next to the woman she loved and saying "I do" would soon be a reality. On that day love won the battle.

There was the usual excitement in the air about the impending wedding that would take place in the backyard that day. The sisters were upstairs in Ruby's room, Ruby nervously trying to figure out what she would wear. Ada was sitting on the bed, watching her sister bring out all of her best dresses and laying them on the bed next to her.

"Which dress do you like best, sister?"

Ada briefly looked at all the dresses lined up on the bed. "Are you sure about this, Ruby? What are your intentions after such a wedding? Are you going to move away from Papa and the farm? What will change because of it?"

"I suppose nothing will change. Nothing will ever change around here. I will never really be free to love who I want. Maybe I'll move far away from this place, to Portland, and start a new life with Ella. Maybe I'll marry Arnold Anderson like Papa keeps talking about. Maybe I'll never marry and become an old spinster here on the farm. Sister, I don't know what will happen to me tomorrow or the day after that. The only thing I have is this day. Please, Ada, give me this day."

Ruby sat on the bed next to Ada; she put her head on her sister's shoulder and began to cry. Ada comforted Ruby. "Sister, I do worry for you. I only want to see you happy. If today brings happiness to you, then so be it."

After Sara brought Ella her breakfast, the chums started getting dressed downstairs. Sara asked Ella, "Say, old pal, do you have an extra hat with you? I hope you don't mind, but I left my best suit and hat at home. Had I known I'd be attending a wedding today I certainly would have been properly prepared."

Ella started laughing. "You and me both. I was only going to be here long enough to visit with Ruby and attend a linen party before going back to work next week."

"Linen party! Who is leaving the group now?" Sara asked.

As Ella buttoned her white gentleman's shirt, she told Sara, "Mildred Taylor from Plover is marrying Willis Thomas in Waupaca next week. I hate spring. We always lose so many of our ladies this time of year."

"What about you and Ruby?" Sara asked.

"What do you mean?" Ella responded as she reached for her tie.

"Will Ruby be joining you in Sheboygan after you two wed?"

Ella stopped tying her tie and looked at Sara. "I don't know what will become of us after this, Sara. Everything in the last two days has happened so fast; I was only thinking about today. Honestly, I don't know what she'll do. I would love nothing more than to have her with me wherever I go. However, she's horribly frightened about upsetting her father, and may never leave this place."

Ruby was still looking at dresses and hadn't noticed that Ada was no longer in the room with her.

"How about this dress?" Ada asked, returning to the room.

"Oh my lord, that's Mama's best dress." Ruby was startled. "Where did you find it? I thought Papa had given all her clothes away, or that Bernice or Dora had it. Sister, I would love to wear it. Do you think she would...?"

Ada smiled. "I think she would love for you to wear it today. When the others were going though her things like a bunch of vultures, I managed to hide this dress in the sewing room. What they don't know won't bother them. Besides, you were Mama's youngest girl. You should have it."

Ruby ran over and gave Ada a hug. "Oh Ada, I miss her so much. Why did she die so soon? I remember when she wore this dress, she looked like a princess. I always wanted to be just like her when I grew up, but I fear I never will be."

Ada grabbed Ruby's shoulders. "Listen, Ruby, you are more like Mama than you'll ever know. You're a strong woman in your own way. This is your day, and she would want you to wear it."

Ruby held the dress up to her chin and looked at herself in the mirror. "I hope it fits me. It will look grand in the photos." Then she stopped. "The photos. Where's Leroy? I haven't seen him all day. I hope he hasn't gone down fishing at the lake."

Ruby called out for him, but there was no response, and she started to panic. Then she called out from her room for Ada and Sara. "Would one of you *please* go and find Leroy and tell him to get the camera set up for us? We cannot have a wedding without photographs."

Sara was still getting dressed, so Ella volunteered to look for Leroy. "I'll go and get the boy. I know where he likes to fish."

Ella breathed in the fresh air, and for a moment enjoyed the solitude as she walked down the path toward the lake. She was relieved to get out of the house for a while, away from the build-up of anxiety from her bride-to-be. While in the house she felt very much like a typical nervous groom. She smiled, thinking how most fellows hated such drama, but she loved every minute of the impending nuptials. She would remember this day like no other. It was a day that the world seemed to change, if only for a moment.

She continued down the path until she saw Leroy walking toward her, with his fishing pole over his right shoulder and a row of fish slung over the other. He was looking down, kicking rocks as he walked, and hadn't noticed Ella standing just a few feet in front of him.

Leroy was startled. "Say, Ella, you just about scared me half to death. What are you doing out here, and why are you all dressed up? Are you two goin' into town? Can I go?" he asked eagerly.

"No, we're not going into town, but we are going to a wedding. Your sister is looking for you. You need to get the camera ready so you can take some pictures."

"Oh boy! I'm going to be the photographer for a wedding. You bet I'll get it ready. Say, who's getting married?"

Ella cleared her throat. "Um, we are. Ruby and me are getting married today. What do you think about that?"

The look on Leroy's face told Ella he was confused. "You two are getting married? But you're both... I mean, but you're not a fella. Well, you look like a fella, but you're not really a fella. Can you do that?" Leroy asked, as he tilted his head to ponder the situation.

Ella knew it was up to her to explain what was going to transpire that day, and she could feel the perspiration starting to run down her back. "Leroy, let me explain. It's very complicated. Well, maybe it's not that complicated. You see, your sister and me love each other. Not like you love your brothers and sisters, but like a man and woman. And, when two people have that kind of love for each other they want to share a life together. They celebrate their love by having a wedding. That's why Ruby and I are having a wedding ceremony today, and we would be honored if you'd be our official photographer. Would you do that for us?"

"Well sure, Ella, that would be swell. Who all's gonna be there?"

"Ada and Sara are here, and the wedding will be in the backyard. But no else can ever know about the wedding. Most people don't understand like you do and they will get angry if they find out. Can you keep this a secret just between us? Not even your papa or friends can find out."

"I suppose, but I don't understand why people would get so angry about it. Boy, it's a good thing I can keep secrets."

"It sure is. I'll race you to the house. The last one there has to clean all those fish." Ella bolted off toward the house before Leroy even realized what she'd wagered.

"Hey, that ain't fair, Ella, you got a head start!" Leroy yelled and started running behind her, fishing pole and all.

Even though Ella had a substantial head start, Leroy was just about to close the gap when Ella touched the back door and proclaimed herself the victor.

"I won," she crowed. Then she noticed Sara and Ada sitting at the kitchen table, drinking lemonade. "Where's Ruby at? She's not down here, is she?" she asked, out of breath. She didn't notice that her once-dapper wool suit was now covered with twigs and dust from her victorious race against Leroy.

"No, she is not, and it's a good thing. You got your suit all dirty," Ada scolded. "If she sees you like this she'll pitch a fit. I suggest you go clean off some of that dirt before the wedding. And Leroy, you need to go and put on some clean clothes, if you have any. You smell like fish. Neither one of you are suitable for a wedding."

Ruby was still upstairs hemming her mother's dress. Her mother had been a full five inches taller than Ruby and she wanted to make sure it fit perfectly. She heard a knock on the door. "Ella, that better not be you," she called out.

"No, it's me, Leroy."

Ruby looked up from her stitching. She suddenly realized that he must know about the wedding, and figured he might have questions. "Come on in, the door is open."

Leroy had already changed into the only clothes he had that didn't smell like fish. His hair was even slicked back with some of his father's pomade, and he had on his best suit jacket over the newest pair of overalls he owned.

"Is this all right to wear to your wedding today, Ruby? The pants that go with the jacket don't fit so well. Daddy said he was going to buy me a new pair the next time he went into town, but he never got around to it."

Ruby knelt down in front of him. "Leroy, you look so handsome. Mama would be so proud of you."

Still, Leroy seemed sad. He was looking down when he asked, "Are ya gonna be leaving me and Pa to live with Ella?"

"No, Leroy, why would you think such a thing?"

"I don't know. I figured because you two are fixin' to get married, you'd be leaving us. Isn't that what married folk do?"

Ruby thought for a moment. "Well, Leroy, I suppose most married couples do, but I'm not ready to move away from you and Papa just yet. Someday I'll leave here, and someday you will too. You'll find that girl you've been dreaming about, with the long brown wavy hair and blue eyes. You'll fall in love and start your own family. But for now we've got to take care of Papa and the farm. Now, are you ready to take some photographs of our wedding?"

"Yes ma'am! Me and the camera are all ready. I even cleaned the lens." Leroy was once again excited about taking the photos, knowing his sister would not be leaving home anytime soon.

"Okay, let me finish fixing this hem. You go wait downstairs with the others. I'll be right down."

TWENTY-SEVEN

For over two hours, Ada, Sara, and Ella sat at the table, patiently waiting for the bride to appear. The clock ticked past 11:30 a.m., and Ruby was still getting ready. They could hear the sound of her shoes nervously pacing the wooden floor above them.

Ella sent Leroy out back to pick some of the best spring flowers he could find. Ada had already washed and trimmed two bundles of flowers and tied string around each one to be used as bouquets for her and the bride. The smaller flowers were cut back and made into simple boutonnières for the chums. She even put the straight pins through them so they would be ready when needed.

An hour had passed since Leroy returned home with the flowers, and now he too sat quietly at the kitchen table, fiddling with the camera while they played the card game 500. Everyone seemed to know that going upstairs to check on Ruby would cause more harm than good.

So all four of them waited patiently.

"Ada, can you come up here please?" They heard Ruby call.

Ada put her cards down and looked around the table at everyone. "I hope this means my sister is finally ready."

As Ada made her way upstairs, Sara looked across the table at Ella. Up to this point Ella had seemed collected in her emotions. However, Sara could tell by Ella's face she was getting nervous about the impending nuptials.

"Say old pal, you're not getting cold feet are you? I would hate to have Leroy bring out his shotgun."

Sara was trying to make light of the situation, but Ella still had a grim look about her.

Ella stood up from the table. "No, I'll be fine. I'm just wondering if Ruby still wants to go through with this wedding. She's been up there for hours. What could possibly be taking her so long?"

Leroy glanced over at Ella and calmly said, "Don't you know by now, girls just take a long time to get ready for anything. I'm only fourteen and I know that."

Ella was comforted by Leroy's young words of wisdom. "I suppose you're right Leroy, I forgot about that."

Just as Ella was going to sit back at the table, she heard the sound of footsteps coming down the stairs, and immediately stood up, her spine straightening.

Ada bounced downstairs and announced, "The bride is ready." Then she ran over to get the flowers from the cooler box.

Leroy jumped up and grabbed the camera as Sara put on her suit jacket. Ella stood and asked, "What do I do now? I've never been in a wedding before, let alone been a groom."

Ada quickly walked over to Ella to pin on her boutonnière. "The gents don't do much. Mostly just stand there and look handsome while the reverend offers a prayer." As soon as Ada said that, she realized they didn't have anyone to offer a prayer for the ceremony.

"Oh my God! Who will offer the prayer for us? How can we have a wedding ceremony without someone saying a prayer?"

Ada shouted up to Ruby, "Sister, you need to wait upstairs a minute. I'll let you know when to come outside."

All three of them stood there for a moment, not knowing what could or should be done. Then Leroy had a brilliant idea. "I know what to do.

Just wait here, I'll be right back." Without another word, he bolted out the back door and ran toward the pastures behind the barn. He was looking for Wallace Henderson.

⚶

Peter Peterson employed Wallace to work full-time on the farm and take care of the maintenance that needed to be done around the place. He was also hired to keep a watchful eye on Ruby and Leroy when their father was out of town. He kept mostly to himself as he quietly went about with his daily chores. However, didn't miss much of what was going on around the farm, or with Ruby.

Wallace had waited for Ruby and Ada to come home from Cora's first party last April. He had seen Elizabeth Fitzgerald remove her hat to reveal her true identity to Ruby in the car outside of their home. He knew Ella was a frequent guest at the family home when Mr. Peterson was out of town. He didn't know what to think about the goings-on with Ruby; he only knew that as long as the kids were home safe and repairs were done, his job was complete and his employment secure.

Wallace never brought up the matter of Ruby's strange visitors with Mr. Peterson. He figured bringing it up would only force his boss to cancel business trips, which could result in him being out of a job.

⚶

Leroy spotted Wallace working on the broken backhoe behind the barn.

"Hey, Wallace, whatcha doing?" Leroy called out.

Wallace heard his name and looked up from the rusted old farm equipment. He pulled out the worn, red cotton handkerchief that had been tucked in the rear pocket of his faded blue overalls and wiped the sweat from his forehead.

"I reckon we'll need this extra hoe by harvest time. I had the men plant two more acres of potatoes this year. But I'm not sure this old thing has it in her to be fixed. What do ya need?"

He could tell Leroy was reconsidering what he was about to ask of him. "I…I mean, we… Well, all of us really. But it's actually for Ruby. Could you say a prayer for her?"

Wallace was alarmed. "Is she ill? What's wrong with her, Leroy?"

Leroy knew his question hadn't come out right. "No, no. Nothin's wrong with her. She's just gettin' married today, and we were wondering if you could give the prayer at the wedding."

"What? Ruby's getting married today? To who? Why isn't your father and the rest of your family here for this? Leroy, are you sure you have your story straight? Maybe I need to get to the house to figure out what's going on around here."

Leroy could tell Wallace was annoyed at not understanding what he was being asked to do. "Yes, sir," he said, and he followed Wallace over to the house.

Ada heard Ruby calling for her from the top of the stairs and rushed to find out what she needed.

"How do I look, sister?" She beamed. "I hemmed Mama's dress the best I could under the circumstances."

Ada stood for a moment. "You look beautiful, Ruby. You look so much like Mama standing there in her dress. She'd be so happy knowing you are wearing it."

Ruby looked down at the dress one last time before going downstairs. "I hope so. Is everything all right down there?" she asked suspiciously, sensing something was wrong.

Ada was standing in the doorway to block Ruby from leaving. "Um, we forgot something, but Leroy's working on it."

A shot of panic went though Ruby. "Forgot what? What does Leroy need to work on?"

Just then, Ada looked out the side window and saw Leroy and Wallace walking from the barn toward the backyard.

"Ruby, go back into your room. I'll let you know when to come down."

In a surge of panic, Ada called out from upstairs window, "Leroy Peterson, come up here. Now!"

Leroy could tell by Ada's tone that she was upset, and had his explanation ready by the time they met halfway up the stairs. "Don't be mad, sister. We can trust Wallace. He's my best friend, and if I ask him to keep a secret, I'm sure he will. Besides, he knows the Bible real good."

"Good heavens Leroy, what were you thinking? Don't you understand we could all get in a lot of trouble if anyone found out what we're doing here today?"

There was a look of disappointment and fear in Leroy's eyes as he glanced down, knowing what he had to tell Ada next would upset her further. "It's too late," he said faintly. "I already told him that Ruby was getting married today. He's here to find out what's going on. I'm sorry, Ada. I thought we needed him to say a wedding prayer for Ruby and Ella."

Ada had little time to react, because when she looked up she saw Wallace walking directly toward the house. He was only steps away from being in the kitchen. She hurried downstairs to intercept him, but it was too late.

He walked into the kitchen and looked at Ella and Sara, still playing cards at the table, dressed in their gentlemen's attire. They both froze when they saw Wallace, not knowing what to say or what to expect from him.

"You?" he blurted. "What in the world is going on around here? Where's Ruby?"

Ella stood up from the table at attention, preparing to answer Wallace' question in her deepest voice, hoping he wouldn't realize she wasn't a man.

Just as Ella cleared her throat to speak, Ada walked into the kitchen and said in the cheeriest voice she could muster, "Say, Wallace, we were hoping you could help us with a little something today."

With a look of bewilderment Wallace responded, "Sure, Miss Ada, you know I'm here to help you kids any way I can, but I'm still not sure what you all need me for. Leroy said something about doing a prayer for Ruby because she is getting married. Is that true, Ada?"

Ada knew that what she was about to ask of Wallace would be difficult to explain, and very likely impossible for him to understand. She squared her shoulders and looked around the room at everyone. "Yes, it is true, Wallace. My baby sister is getting married today to Mr. O'Brien right here," she said, pointing to Ella. "I'm going to be the maid of honor, Leroy is going to be the photographer, and our friend here, Sara, is going to be Mr. O'Brien's best man."

Ada could tell that Wallace was baffled about what he was hearing; she could see little beads of sweat starting to form on his forehead. He once again took out his handkerchief to wipe his brow and started nervously scratching his head.

"Ada, I sure don't know what you all are doing here or how I can help. I thought he was a she, or she was a he. You see. I don't even know who's who around here. I think it's best I leave you all and get back to working on that broken-down old hoe."

As Wallace put on his hat to leave, Ella spoke up. "No, wait please, Wallace. We're rehearsing for a play we'll be doing in Almond in the next few weeks. The young gentlemen in the play with us cannot possibly drive out this far, that's why my friend and I are dressed up as gents. The play is called 'Henpecked Henry,' and we couldn't possibly go on rehearsing without someone playing the reverend. It's the most important scene in the play."

Ada glanced over to Ella and picked up on what she was doing. "Yes, Wallace, of course we're doing a play. What else would they be doing dressed like this? So, could you be a doll and help us out? It will only take a few minutes of your time, and then you can go back to working on that old hoe of ours. What do you say?"

Leroy piped in, "Wallace, you know the Bible better than anyone I know. You would be a perfect preacher man. I bet you can act real good too."

Wallace took off his hat again to scratch the top of his head. "A play? You all mean to tell me that you've been working on a play all this time?" He stopped again, trying to decide if what they were telling him was true. Finally he said slowly, "Well, I have been in a few church plays, and folks tell me I was the best Moses they ever had. But I don't have all day, you know."

Sara broke her silence. "No sir, it should only take about ten minutes. Then you'll be done with us, and we won't bother you for the rest of the day. I promise."

"Alright, then. Let's get on with it. Just tell me what I need to do so you all can leave me to my work," he told the group begrudgingly.

Ada grabbed Wallace and hugged him.

"Oh, Wallace, that's grand of you. Let me go tell Ruby, she'll be so happy knowing you'll be joining us today for rehearsal."

Ada ran upstairs to tell Ruby. "Sister, we're finally ready for you. We will be waiting for you out back by the garden. Oh, and don't be concerned if you see Wallace with us."

"Why in the world is Wallace here? You know the only reason he's on this farm is to sneak around checking us. What if he tells Papa?"

"He won't say a word to anyone. He thinks we're only rehearsing for a play we're doing."

Ruby was confused. "A play?"

"Yes, a play. Just go along with it. Everything will be fine, but we don't have much time. He won't suspect a thing. Now wait five minutes and then join us out back in the garden." Ada looked over her shoulder one last time before quickly heading outside with the others. "Ruby, you look so lovely."

TWENTY-EIGHT

It was 2:00 p.m. by the time the wedding party walked toward the garden in the backyard. Ella was only steps away from making her wedding dreams into a reality. She was also preparing herself for the performance of her lifetime. She had been in the drama club in college, even acting in some plays, but nothing like this. She wasn't sure that their plan to convince Wallace that the ceremony was simply part of a play was going to work.

Ella was relieved to finally be walking toward the garden. She was leading the group, and stopped for a moment to call out, "I think this would be a perfect spot, underneath these two trees."

The wedding party joined her in an area just in front of two elm trees, next to the garden of spring flowers that overlooked the rolling hillside of the farm. Ella was relieved to see Ada as she approached the group. There was uncertainty in her eyes until Ada clapped her hands together.

"Alright everyone, listen up: You all know your lines. We must get in our positions. The bride will be joining us any minute, and we must be ready."

Ada looked to Ella for assistance. "Yes, indeed," Ella said. "Let's get ready. Sara, since you are acting as my best man, you will be standing just to my left. Ada, you are playing the role of the matron of honor, so please stand to the right side of the bride. Dear Wallace, please stand next to the best man. Leroy, you can stand next to Ada. I, of course, will be playing the role of the groom, and will be standing next to the bride."

Just as everyone got into position, Ella saw the back door open. She could hardly breathe as Ruby started walking toward her. Her mind had been full of thoughts up until that moment: now, everything vanished. She could no longer hear the birds chirping in the trees, or feel the high after-noon sun on her skin. Her senses deadened to everything except the sight of Ruby walking toward her in her wedding dress and veil. The veil was made from a lace tablecloth that had yellowed with age.

Ruby looked down as she nervously walked toward the group, grip-ping the small bouquet of flowers. Then, as she moved closer, she looked up and saw everything she had hoped for. She saw Ella looking directly into her eyes, and she could feel her emotions rising.

When Ruby was only a couple of feet away from her Ella, Ada approached and took the bouquet from her hands. "Wallace, would you be so kind as to lead the bride the rest of the way next to the groom?"

Wallace nervously agreed. "Yes, ma'am. What do I do after that? Are there any lines you want me to read from the play?"

Ada instructed him carefully. "Once the bride takes the hand of the groom you need to offer a prayer for the couple. Any prayer will do. Once you're done, the couple will exchange vows. They've already memorized their lines, so you won't need to do anything at all. After they're done, Leroy will take some photographs and you can go back to fixing the backhoe."

While Ada explained to Wallace what his role was, Ruby and Ella stood only a few feet apart, bashfully smiling at each other the way two people do when they are in love and about to marry.

Ada looked over her left shoulder and asked, "Sara, Leroy, Ruby and Ella, do you all know your lines?" They all responded by nodding their heads in unison.

"Very well then, let's get on with it, shall we?"

They all nodded again.

Wallace approached Ruby and extended his arm for her to hold onto. He walked her forward slowly and gently placed her shoulder-to-shoulder with Ella. As he stood before them both, he removed his old dusty working hat as a sign of respect.

They all bowed their heads to pray. Wallace centered himself, and then delivered the best prayer he could think of on such sort notice.

"Dear Lord, thank you for this beautiful day we have. Thank you for the warmth of the sun that helps our fields to become abundant with food. We stand before you and ask that you bless all of us standing here today. We also ask, dear Lord, that you hold in your hand and protect this...um, this man?" Wallace was unsure how to address Ella, or what to say for a moment.

Ada leaned in and whispered, "The name of the character is Mr. O'Brien. Just pretend Ella's a gent and you'll do fine."

"Very well then," he answered. "We ask, dear Lord, we ask that you hold in your hands and protect Mr. O'Brien and his bride, Ruby, in holy marriage today and supply them with strong healthy children some-day. Amen."

While all their heads were still bowed, Leroy started snickering a little. Ada gave him a swift kick to the side of his leg.

"Ouch," Leroy moaned quietly.

"That was real nice," Ada told Wallace as he took one step back.

Ruby and Ella were now facing each other. Ella reached to hold Ruby's hand in hers before she spoke. "My dearest, I love you with all my heart, and will protect you now and forever. If you cry, I will be there to wipe your tears and to offer my shoulder for support. If you are ill, I will be there to hold your hand until you are well. When you laugh, we will laugh together as one. I do swear. I do."

Ruby looked into Ella's eyes and saw the tears of happiness she was trying desperately not to release. Ruby paused a moment for Ella to compose herself; then it was her turn.

"My darling, you have opened my heart in ways I never thought possible. I had never known such happiness existed until you came into my life. You are strong where I am weak. You are the voice of reason when I am confused. You will forever hold my heart in the palm of your hand, as I will always hold yours. I do love you. I do."

Sara then took off one of her own rings and handed it to Ella to place on Ruby's ring finger. It was one of Sara's favorite rings: a silver one in the shape of a peacock, inlaid with light-blue stones.

As Ella placed the ring on Ruby's ring finger, Ella smiled and said one more time, "I do."

Ella placed only a quick kiss on Ruby's check, fearing Wallace had seen enough for one day.

Leroy had loads of fun taking photos and making sure everyone looked their best for the blessed event. Wallace was even convinced to get into the act, as he and Ella lifted Leroy from the ground while the boy sat inside a water bucket.

The wedding ceremony that took place that day went unannounced to outsiders. The stakes were too high. Not even the ladies and chums in Cora's group could be trusted with the joyous news, because such an event would surely be talked about. However, Ruby and Ella knew. The ground they stood on and the songbirds flying above them knew. So did the elm trees that provided shade from the hot sun. It was a marriage that would only be felt in their hearts and captured in photographs.

Our Wedding: Ada, Ella, Ruby and Sara Chums: Ella and Sara

Soft-Water: Ella, Leroy and Wallace

"Pals" Ella and Sara

*Top: Ella and Ruby -
Bottom: Ella as Mr. O'Brien*

TWENTY-NINE

August 18, 1915

Ella spent the remainder of that summer working side by side with Ruby on the farm, and as promised, the subject of moving to Oregon was not discussed. However, it was never far from either of their thoughts. Ruby's father was due home any day, and Ella could tell by the aching pit in her stomach that she too needed to return to Sheboygan to resume her teaching. There was a sad silence in the house the day before her return home. Both of them were still unsure what effect, if any, the wedding would have on their lives.

The day before Ella was to leave, Ruby prepared food for a backyard picnic and walked out back to get everything set up. She unfolded the blanket underneath the elm trees, and realized it was the same spot where a little over two months ago their wedding ceremony had been held. It seemed like such a long time ago—so long ago it felt as if it were a dream.

Ruby picked some pink wildflowers and arranged them neatly in a Mason jar, which she placed next to the chicken pie and peach preserves. Once she was satisfied the setting was perfect, she poured herself a glass of lemonade and sat alone, looking up at the sky and waiting for Ella to join her. The clouds were pure white and looked like plumes of cotton hanging from the clear blue sky. To keep her mind from dwelling on Ella leaving, she looked for shapes and faces within them.

Soon Ella walked from the house to join Ruby for the picnic. As she approached, she could tell what Ruby was doing, watching the clouds so intently. Ella smiled at her beauty, loving the fact that Ruby enjoyed such simple pleasures. Her eyes swelled with tears of joy and sorrow. Her heart was heavy, not knowing when they would see each other next.

She was not wearing her gentlemen's clothing—instead she had on a dark gray dress skirt and a white cotton shirt, with a colorful silk scarf tied around her neck. As much as Ella hated wearing dresses, she knew how difficult the transition from Mr. O'Brien to Miss Karnopp would be on the first day back to teaching Monday morning. She always hoped a more gradual approach would alleviate some of her discomfort, but it never did.

Ella stepped on a twig, breaking Ruby's concentration on the billowing clouds above. When Ruby turned around, she saw that Ella was wearing a dress. She wasn't accustomed to seeing Ella in ladies' clothes, and while surprised by it, she was excited to see her. "My, my, Miss Karnopp, you can be my teacher anytime. Please let me take one last photo of you before we start eating."

With Ruby's encouragement Ella climbed to the top of one of the boulders next to the tree line. "How do you ladies manage to climb trees and rocks in a dress?" Ella asked, pushing the hair from her face.

Ruby was amused at how difficult it was for Ella to climb the boulder but promised herself she wouldn't laugh. "You see? It's not that easy. Maybe next time we go camping you and your pals won't call us slowpokes."

Ella felt her checks getting warm and knew it had nothing to do with the summer sun. She looked down with a schoolgirl smile and waited for Ruby to take her picture. She didn't care that some of her hair had come undone from her loosely pinned bun; she was determined to give Ruby a photo to remember.

Once she hopped off the boulder, Ella looked down at the assortment of food and noticed the charred edges of the cornbread and pie. It reminded her of the first meal Ruby had prepared, and the kissing crust of the bread that brought them together.

That afternoon, after they had their fill of picnic food and pie, they lay down on the blanket next to each other to look up to the sky. Both were now looking for different faces and animals as the cauliflower-like cloud formations slowly changed shapes. Hand in hand, they fell asleep on the small piece of land that would forever keep their secret.

The next morning, Ella prepared to leave after breakfast, dressed in her gentleman's driving attire. They both ate quietly, sitting with the reality of her departure. The silence between them was foreign and awkward: a mixture of sadness and not knowing what would come next. Neither of them was hungry, and they avoided looking at each other for fear of crying.

Ruby broke the silence. "When should I expect to see you again?"

Ella looked down at her plate. "I'll pay you a visit on my next school break, if you have no plans?"

Ruby was irritated that Ella would think to ask if she had other plans. "I won't have plans, Ella. You only need to tell me that you will be here, and that's what my plans will be."

Ella was still looking down at the eggs on her plate. "Have you had second thoughts about what happened between us this summer? Have you thought at all about moving to Portland with me?"

Ruby could feel her eyes starting to burn from the tears she was trying not to shed, but there was no holding them back. "Ella, if I had this summer to do over again I would do nothing differently. If I could leave here with you today, I swear I would. But Leroy and my father need me. It's only been three years since Mother passed. I couldn't live with myself if something happened to either of them. I hope you understand that I need more time before I can leave."

Ella looked up and reached for Ruby's hand.

"My love, I do understand. If you need more time, you shall have it. I just wish we didn't need to be apart. I would love nothing more than to wake up to you each morning and fall asleep with you every night for the rest of my life. But that would be selfish of me. I promise I will visit you whenever I can, and we'll hold each other's hearts in our hands until then."

With the thought of being apart, they held each other tightly and pledged their love one last time. Ella could barely contain her emotions at leaving Ruby. As she was driving away, she looked over her shoulder to see Ruby standing in a cloud of dust in the driveway. With a tip of her hat, she was on her way.

Ella bursting – August 18, 1915

THIRTY

Fall 1915

Peter Peterson returned home mid-September, and he did not arrive empty-handed. During his extended business travels he had purchased five additional Holstein cows. However, Ruby had no reason to celebrate his procurement, because it meant more time taking care of the livestock, and less time to have fun visiting with the ladies and chums.

By the end of October the potatoes had already been harvested, but as always, there was still work to be done. In early November, an Indian summer heat wave enveloped the farm. It was warm in Ruby's room, even after the sun had long since set. There was no escaping the rising heat in her second-story bedroom. Ruby wrapped a cool piece of cloth around the back of her neck, hoping that at some point a breeze would find its way through one of the open windows to offer relief.

Her only reprieve from discomfort was looking at her cherished photos. Ruby smiled as she lifted each of the wedding photos to the light, thinking about how free she'd felt that June day, and how happy she and Ella were that summer. It seemed like such a long time since their wedding vows, yet she could still feel Ella's touch on her skin. She decided the photos should be placed in her picture book along with her collection of family and friends. The picture book was her personal diary of every cherished person and moment in her young life. It was for her eyes only, hidden in plain sight, though nobody but Ada or Ella ever dared go into her room.

She opened the book to the next available space, looking for the perfect spot on the heavy black pages. She arranged the photos to make sure they would fit before applying glue to cement them in their permanent location. Pleased with the newest additions, she used her favorite white-ink fountain pen to write the caption: 'Our Wedding.'

It wasn't uncommon for Peter Peterson to question Wallace about the activity on the farm when he returned home from one of his extended business trips. He inquired first about the potatoes and cows, but his questions would inevitably turn to finding out if Ruby had any gentlemen callers over the summer, hoping someday Ruby would take an interest in a boy and settle down.

Wallace had a strange look on his face as he replied, "No, not really."

Mr. Peterson wasn't at all satisfied with that answer. "What does that mean, Wallace? Was there a gentleman suitor calling on Ruby or not?"

"Well, there were some visitors here for Miss Ruby in June. But it turned out they was only girls dressed as men."

"What are you talking about, Wallace? What you're saying makes no sense at all."

Wallace could tell Mr. Peterson was getting annoyed, and took a step back before explaining, "Ya see, I thought one of Ruby's friends was a fellow, but it was actually a girl dressed as a gent. I guess they was rehearsing for a play they were doing. I even helped them by playing the role of the preacher man."

With that bit of news, Peter Peterson walked away and found a chair in the shade, where he quietly sat down. He sat there, not knowing what to think about his youngest daughter. He worried so about her. She seemed so different from his other eight kids. Now he worried that she might be doing something 'unnatural' with her summer visitors. He had no knowledge of any such play, and suspected she had pulled one over on Wallace. He had heard of such things, unnatural things, happening in the big city, but he never imagined anything like that occurring to his family on his small farm.

Peter sat there a while longer, gazing at his house and wishing he had the guidance of his beloved wife, Hilda. He feared he had failed as a father, and that somehow he was to blame for Ruby's behavior. He never brought up the subject with Ruby, but he became determined that if his daughter was not interested in finding a man, he would find one for her. He had been considering selling the farm, since selling insurance was becoming much more lucrative than selling potatoes. And now, besides worrying about the farm, managing his youngest was becoming much more difficult.

THIRTY-ONE

December 1915

Since the wedding, Ruby and Ella had seen each other only a few times. Both were eager for the Christmas holiday, when they would have the whole week to be together. Five days before Christmas, while Ruby and Leroy were decorating the house with garlands and mistletoe, there was a knock at the door. Ruby hoped it was Ella, but instead a telegram delivery boy stood outside the door, eager to collect a tip.

After seeing the telegram was from Ella, she quickly gave the boy a few coins and rushed upstairs to her room to read it.

Dearest Pete, I am afraid I have bad news for you. I took a terrible fall two days ago and suffered a head injury. My doctor has advised me not to return to work or travel for the next two weeks. I am sorry to disappoint you and Leroy, but I won't be able to see you for Christmas. I hope you understand it is not safe right now.

Ella

Ruby was of course worried when she read the news of Ella's injury, and noticed that the note itself seemed disconnected and devoid of emotion, unlike Ella's other letters. She wished she had access to a phone so she could hear Ella's voice. *Maybe it's because she's seriously injured,* Ruby thought with a sickening pain in her stomach. She read the letter again, and became frightened by the last words in the telegram. *What did she mean, 'it is not safe right now'?*

Ruby's stomach started to churn, wondering if the injury Ella had suffered was from more than a simple fall.

Indeed, Ruby was right. There was no accidental fall down the stairs. Ella was attacked by three men outside of her apartment. One of the men was a neighbor, who'd seen Ella leaving her home in her gentlemen's driving attire one weekend. He reported witnessing the 'unnatural act' to his friends at a downtown Sheboygan bar.

One night after drinking heavily, the three men waited for Ella to return home, where they brutally attacked her with a baseball bat, hitting her in the head. The blow dropped her to the ground like a lead balloon. Her body hit the cold hard ground just a few feet away from the stairs leading to her apartment. She felt the warm blood trickling down the left side of her face, but wasn't sure right away what had happened. Trying to gather her thoughts, she heard the men laughing and realized her fall was no accident. The shooting pain in her head was overtaken by waves of fear. She wondered what would be coming next.

As she struggled to maintain consciousness, one of the men grabbed her by her hair and told her, "German teacher, you best listen up good. We don't want you teaching our children how to be German, and we damn well don't want you teaching our girls how to dress up as boys. You best repent for your sins. And don't you dare tell the police about us or what happened here tonight, because if you do, we will come back for you, and next time you won't be left alive."

Even through the ringing in her ears Ella could hear the hatred in his voice and smell the whiskey on his breath, but she could fight no longer. She felt herself drifting into the darkness of unconsciousness. Twenty minutes went by, and then Ella heard people talking around her. She wasn't sure where she was, but knew she must have passed out after the men left.

A passerby had noticed Ella's lifeless body on the ground at the bottom of the stairs, and summoned a doctor to her home. She felt the weight of her legs dangling just inches off the ground and pressure under her arms as some of her neighbors carried her up the stairs and into the safety of her apartment. She heard some of the people standing around whispering that she must have slipped and fallen on the ice.

Finally, a car sputtered up the street and stopped in front of the apartment. It was the doctor: a tall, skinny man who arrived wearing a suit jacket that looked five sizes too small. His clothing was disheveled, his silver hair uncombed.

When the doctor arrived, he found Ella sitting on her couch holding a rag to her head to stop the bleeding. He recognized her as being one of the high school teachers in town. "Good evening, miss. What happened to you tonight?"

Ella watched the doctor as he opened his black leather medical bag to pull out his stethoscope. Before saying a word, she remembered what she'd been told by one of the attackers. She thought for a moment before slowly responding, "I must have fallen down the steps and hit my head on the ground." Her voice was weak and shaken.

The doctor removed the crimson-colored rag and examined her head to identify where the blood was coming from. Then he looked into her eyes to check her pupils. "You say you fell. Are you sure about that, miss? With a bump on top of your head like that, it looks like you got hit by something, or someone."

"No, doctor, I can assure you I must have stepped on a patch of ice at the top of my stairs and fallen all the way to the bottom," Ella said adamantly, but without making eye contact.

"Very well, miss. You will need some stitches, and you may have a concussion. Let's get you over to my office so I can clean this cut out and get you all fixed up."

Ella was hesitant to go with the doctor, but when she stood up she could feel her legs start to buckle and her head begin to pound. The doctor and another woman led Ella to his car. As the doctor drove to his office, she sat in the back seat wondering if one of the men standing along the side of the street was one of her attackers. She hadn't gotten a good look at them, but the laughter of one of the men seemed all too familiar to her.

She hated feeling so helpless and vulnerable, but most of all she hated the fear those men instilled in her. They clearly knew where she lived and worked. They knew about her weekend gentlemen's attire. Then she thought, *What else do they know? What if any of them found out about Ruby and me? What if someone found the wedding photos? What would they do to us?*

After Ella received eight stitches, the good doctor delivered her back to her apartment. He offered to assist her up the stairs, but Ella insisted she was well enough to make it on her own. Before the doctor drove away, he told her, "Please be careful, Miss Ella. We don't want you to take another nasty fall." She looked over her shoulder at him, unsure if his statement was one of concern, or a warning.

As she walked up to her front door, Ella flashed back to what had happened only hours ago on the stairs below. As soon as she entered her home, she locked the door behind her and began composing a telegram to warn Ruby. Convinced that all of her actions were now under scrutiny by the locals, she chose her words carefully so as not to raise suspicions.

Two weeks had passed since the attack, and Ella was still suffering from migraines as a result of her injuries. She was desperate to get a more detailed letter out to Ruby explaining what had happened. However, she was fearful that someone at the local post office would open and read any mail she sent. Instead, she had one of her teacher friends send a letter to Ruby from a nearby town, with an unfamiliar return name and address on it.

Initially Ruby was confused by the letter, but to her horror quickly learned the real cause of her beloved Ella's head injury. She had heard of such attacks, but never thought Ella or any of her friends would be caught. Ella begged Ruby to stay away until she was sure it was safe for them to make contact again. Ruby was heartbroken by Ella's request, but now fully understood how dangerous their love was.

Months had passed since Ella sent the letter to Ruby, and since she had not received any letters or telegrams from Ruby, it seemed as if her message to be safe was understood.

Sheboygan Press (Sheboygan, Wisconsin)
December 22, 1915

Miss Ella Karnopp, head of the German department at the high school is suffering from injuries recently sustained during a fall. She has not been able to attend to her duties at the school for several days.

THIRTY-TWO

In the early 1900s, society viewed single women and single men in vastly different ways. Women who were still single after twenty-five were considered old maids or spinsters. These unmarried women were mostly well-educated and worked as teachers, nurses, or in other professions that served the betterment of the community. Although this lifestyle was not condoned, there was a far less negative connotation associated with a husbandless woman compared to a wifeless man, unless he was a priest.

With a flood of immigrants traveling to the United States during the First Great Migration (1910-1930), Christian conservative groups believed the new European arrivals lacked their same moral fiber. By the time war was declared on April 2, 1917, the National Purity Party (NPP) had begun drafting a bill to gain control of 'social morality' and maintain 'family values.'

With the wave of hyper-patriotism and fear of Communism in the U.S., it was the perfect time for the NPP to instill their own sense of what 'American values' should be. They capitalized on it by introducing the Sedition Act, which was passed into law on May 16, 1918, during an era that was considered the First Red Scare.

Initially, the new law looked quite reasonable. The Sedition Act was supposedly designed to protect our men in the military from protestors and unpatriotic domestic attacks. However, there was a darker intent—censorship—which worked hand-in-hand with Mr. Comstock, and his Act which also allowed legal censorship of U.S. Mail.

It was no coincidence that both laws were written by the same organization, called the Christian Morality Group (CMG). Both laws allowed the postmaster general to routinely open mail, and refuse or impound delivery of materials which were deemed disloyal, profane, or abusive toward the United States.

Morality groups presumed that immigrants were 'deviant' because a large number of them lived in big cities, where most rumors of homosexual activity occurred. The CMG and the federal government used this new law to deepen their search for erotic or homosexual materials and correspondence. Blending the two laws together, they managed to spin a platform that equated homosexuality with being disloyal and a danger to the American way of life. This further propelled the notion that every man and woman must be married and have children to be considered a 'good American.'

To go a step further, in 1919 a book was written by B.G. Jefferis called *Searchlights on Health: The Science of Eugenics*. In his book, Jefferis referred to childless people as 'deplorable.' He also stated that it was a "scientific fact that young people that dislike the care and confinement of children and prefer society and social entertainments do great injury to their health. And women that have a dozen or more children have better health than before marriage."

I can't fathom what went though the mind of any person reading or hearing such things back then. I can only imagine the fear, panic, and self-hatred a woman might experience if she did not want a life based on this script for the 'American way of life.'

THIRTY-THREE

In 1915, people talked mostly about the war with Germany spreading throughout Europe. Although the United States had not yet entered World War I, there was a billowing of hatred for Germany and its ruler, Kaiser Wilhelm. Most residents in Amherst were immigrants from Germany and Scandinavian countries, who had left their homelands to get away from war. Now it seemed as if the great land of America was heading in the direction so many wanted to leave behind.

Parades down Main Street were taking place on a weekly basis, in support of the United States going to war in France to stop the evils of Germany. There were cheers and jeers from spectators as they watched a replica of Kaiser Wilhelm (also referred to simply as 'The Kaiser'), hanging from a noose as it passed down Main Street. Signifying their hatred of the notorious German, the rag replica was set ablaze at the end of the parade, to the glee of the crowd.

The biggest change for Ruby came in the spring of 1916, when Peter Peterson decided to sell the family farm and move into a home he'd purchased in Amherst Village. At the age of fifty-six, he'd grown tired of tending to the farm and the constant worry about how much the crops would produce. Besides, selling insurance was far less labor-intensive, and the income much more reliable. He was still required to travel a great deal, but he figured with Ruby living in town she would have a greater chance of finding a suitable husband.

He blamed himself for the fact that Ruby hadn't yet met a man. Maybe it was because she was stuck out on the farm, he thought. He even bought an extra car for her, but she considered it unladylike and never learned how to drive. If she needed to go anywhere, Leroy or someone else would be more than happy to motor her to her destination.

Ruby had mixed emotions about moving into town. She was excited by the prospect of living closer to her friends and social activities. Also, since she and Ella were now able to communicate again, the train station would be much more convenient for her visits. However, the idea of leaving the farm, the only home she had ever known, was daunting.

As she was slowly packing her belongings, memories of her mother, and of the wonderful things that had happened in her little home, flooded her thoughts. She looked at her photo album, and then glanced at the backyard where her wedding to Ella had taken place the year before. She replayed that New Year's Eve morning in her mind, remembering waking Ella with the news that they were snowed in, and how they'd dressed up to play in the snow so Leroy could take photos. She even thought she might miss waking up at the crack of dawn to milk the cows.

Looking out her window, Ruby could see her world changing before her eyes. She wondered what would come her way next.

Leroy was fifteen now, and strong enough to lift some of the biggest pieces of furniture. She watched him and their older brother, Elmer, as they placed their mother's armchair in the back of their horse-drawn flatbed wagon. Ada had come home to help the family move and to deliver the news that she and Charles would be getting married in June of the coming year and moving to Stevens Point.

"Come on, sister! Are you going to help us or just stand there looking out the window all day?" Elmer called out to Ruby with sweat running down his face.

Ruby quickly wrapped a blanket around her photo album and hid it at the bottom of a wooden crate, underneath some of her clothing.

"Hold your horses, Elmer, I'm almost done!" she yelled back.

"That's good, since you had weeks to do your packing. You should be done already."

Ada came to the defense of her sister. "Now Elmer, don't be so hard on her. It's the first time she has ever had to move. She's lived here for twenty years, and this can't be easy for her."

Elmer released his grip on a heavy box of books. As it hit the floor with a loud bang, he could contain himself no more. "Easy! She's had it easier than any of us. Pa just keeps on making excuses for her. She hasn't taken a husband yet. What is she going to do when she gets out into the real world? What is she going to do now that she doesn't have any chores to do around the farm? She doesn't have a way to make a living. The only thing she's good at is milking cows. She better start looking for a fellow fast, because at her age, people are gonna start talking. If they do, then no man will have her."

"Elmer Peterson, you stop that right now," Ada scolded her older brother. "Just because she hasn't found the right gentleman and has no job, or any skills to speak of, doesn't grant you the right to be mean to her. Besides, Papa told me he's been talking to the Andersons about their son Arnold. He's the same age as Ruby and they have a lot in common. Everyone thinks they would make a lovely couple."

Unbeknownst to Ada and Elmer, Ruby was listening to their conversation from the other room. At first, she was pleased that her sister came to her defense. Then she felt her body grow heavy with the weight of betrayal, hearing that her father was making arrangements with the Anderson family behind her back.

She knew Arnold Anderson—the quiet son of a dairy farmer—but had no romantic interest in him. They had seen each other at a couple of dances, but he seemed too shy to even look at any girl, let alone ask her to dance.

Ruby figured that since there was never an inkling of romance between them, nothing would become of her father's matchmaking attempt. Still, she could feel her throat tightening and her head beginning to ache, just knowing her father and the Andersons were planning behind her back.

THIRTY-FOUR

By the spring of 1917, Ruby had settled into her new home in town nicely. She had a feeling of being connected to the outside world. With the train tracks now only a few hundred feet away, she felt the pounding of the huge locomotive engines and watched the passenger and boxcars as they creaked past her home. It was the sweet melody of freedom: at a moment's notice she could hop on a train and travel wherever she wanted to go.

The new house even had a telephone, although it was a party line, shared with neighbors. Nonetheless, news of events and out-of-town visitors traveled much faster than when she'd relied on letters and telegrams sent to the farm. The world seemed so accessible to her now.

With no farm work to be done, the calluses on Ruby's hands quickly faded. Instead of milking cows and mucking stalls, she was more inclined to spend her days leisurely walking into town, which was now only minutes from home. Even Mrs. Wells, who owned the dress shop, looked forward to their daily visits, as did the other store merchants she stopped to chat with.

Nightly gatherings with the gals at the Opera House were a common occurrence, but only if her father was out of town. The Opera House was located in the center of town. The two-story, light-brown brick building was the heart of Amherst. When bands played, music flooded into the streets from its wide, arched entrance.

It was seemingly a grand time for Ruby, with the exception of frequent visits from the Anderson family, which often included Arnold. With the ever-increasing news of war with Germany and talk of a draft for young American men, the Andersons seemed more intent than ever on seeing them romantically involved.

Ruby knew why the Andersons were there. She didn't dislike Arnold, but they had little in common, and he didn't fit in with the rest of her friends. He was a quiet fellow, and a bit of a loner who only seemed interested in playing baseball with his pals. As far as Ruby knew, he had never had a girlfriend. *Maybe he's too shy, or just not that interested in the ladies,* she thought. Regardless, she had played along with the family's plan for the past few months. She was hoping at some point they would realize that their matchmaking attempt had failed, and discontinue such visits.

THIRTY-FIVE

At the age of sixteen, Leroy traveled to Stevens Point to spend the summer with his older brother, Elmer. He found a job at the local grocery store and was earning good money before school started up again in the fall. Peter Peterson was still on the road much of the time, selling insurance. He paid Ruby two dollars a week to do his bookkeeping and to keep up with the household chores, which was much easier for her to manage without the need to milk cows or concern herself with other farm duties.

Ruby was alone at home most of the time, but she was never lonely. Ella visited during school holidays, though she became more cautious after the assault. Even though Ella had physically healed from her head injury, the hateful words spoken to her that night never left her thoughts.

Ella took extra steps to keep them both safe. To avoid being seen by neighbors, she changed into her gentleman's driving clothing well outside city limits. She discovered an old, abandoned barn next to a burnt-out house just off the highway. She found a place in the barn to store most of her clothing, and hung a mirror on the back of the door to ensure she looked her best before walking outside. When she pulled back onto the road, she was liberated from her long bulky dress and womanly garments. Motoring down the road with a renewed sense of freedom, she smiled and tipped her bowler hat to oncoming drivers as they passed. None of them suspected she was anything other than a friendly gent out for an afternoon drive.

Ella kept her promise to Ruby never to bring up moving to Portland. However, as she drove toward Amherst, the thought weighed heavy on her mind. Ella allowed herself the pleasure of thinking maybe this would be the visit when Ruby would fully commit and agree to move with her to Portland.

THIRTY-SIX

Arnold was the same age as Ruby, and he too was avoiding marriage as long as possible. He was working as a cattle-hand on a small farm an hour outside of town. Unaware of the plans both families had for him and Ruby, he enjoyed living on the farm and playing baseball or spending time with his gentleman friends whenever he wanted. He knew marriage and children were expected of him, but he didn't fancy himself to be much of a ladies' man.

The thought of war was on the minds of most people back then, especially Arnold and other young men his age. At twenty-one, he knew he would surely be called to duty if the U.S. entered into war. But until then, he was content living his single life on the farm.

With war declared against Germany on April 2, 1917, all men between the ages of twenty-one and thirty-one were required to register for military service. Arnold, along with thousands of other young men, registered on June 5, 1917. The next week he returned home to be with his family in Amherst. Being that he was their only son, the Andersons prayed Arnold would not be chosen in the national lottery. However, their prayers went unanswered—a telegram arrived on September 1, 1917, informing Arnold his name had been pulled in the draft lottery. He was to report to Camp Great in Illinois on December 1, 1917, to receive military training before heading to France.

Once Arnold received his orders to report for duty, both families were resolved that Ruby and Arnold would become husband and wife before he headed to France. The Andersons wanted the marriage to occur before their son left for military training. After all, how would it look if the poor lad didn't have a sweetheart back home to write letters to?

"Papa, how could you?" Ruby screamed out. "Why do you and the Andersons insist that Arnold and me get married? We don't have anything in common. When he comes over we barely talk. He held my hand once and his palm was so sweaty I had to wipe if off on the couch."

Peter Peterson had fire in his eyes and his voice rose. "Listen to me, Ruby Sarah Peterson. I've given you every opportunity to find your own husband. I even moved into town so you could meet some nice fella. But all you do is spend time with your lady friends, and some of them don't even look like ladies. You don't want to go back to school to become a teacher, and you don't have any job to speak of. I can't keep taking care of you. If your mother were here she would tell you the same darn thing. So stop resisting me on this. The Andersons are a good family and Arnold is a good man. They're heartbroken their son is going to war and may never return. It's our patriotic duty to make sure the boys over in France have someone worth killing and living for while they're fighting the Germans and protecting our country. Arnold needs someone to come home to, and Ruby, that person is you. Besides, you're both getting too old not to be married."

Ruby's father had never been so forceful with her. She was silent for a moment, collecting her thoughts. She knew better than to continue the debate with him. Arnold was to report to Camp Grant in the next few months, and writing an occasional letter to him wouldn't be all that bad. As long as she wasn't required to marry him before he left for training. After all, the war could go on for years. *It might be five years or more before he comes home,* she thought. She kept herself from thinking the most morbid thought—that he might not return at all.

"Fine, Papa. I'll do it. I'll marry Arnold for you and my country. But I will only marry him once he returns from the war, not before. He can consider me his fiancée and I will do my part by keeping his spirits up by writing him letters. But that's it."

Her father's face was still red from frustration, but he seemed satisfied that Ruby had finally agreed. Before leaving the house he told Ruby, "Very well then. I'll inform the Andersons."

Ruby was alone with her thoughts in the house. *Well, there it is then. I've finally done it. I hope everyone is happy now,* Ruby said to herself as she sat in her mother's chair. She watched the multi-colored reflections of sunlight spilling through the crescent stained-glass window onto the parlor floor. She tried to imagine what words of comfort her mother might have for her this time. *Mama, is this what you want, too?*

She hoped once again for a response from her mother, but heard only the sound of the ticking clock over the fireplace. It seemed to be getting louder and louder with each passing moment.

THIRTY-SEVEN

It had been a week since Ruby agreed to marry Arnold. However, Mr. Peterson had yet to inform the Andersons of Ruby's conditional agreement to marry their son. He was sorry for the harsh tone he'd taken with his daughter, but he knew it was something that needed to be done. There were few words between them, because Ruby spent that week in her room contemplating what she should or could do next, barely coming downstairs to eat. Peter resigned himself to taking his meals at the local restaurant, since Ruby was on a silent, unofficial strike. No housecleaning, cooking, or bookkeeping had been done since their last conversation.

On the eighth day, Ruby heard a knock on the front door. She went downstairs to find out who it was, and stopped dead in her tracks when she saw, through the side window, Alfred and Christina Anderson standing at her front door. *What are they doing here?* she thought. She wasn't sure if her father was at home, and she figured if she hid behind the couch the Andersons would leave. Then she heard her father's footsteps heading toward the door. Ruby ran upstairs to her room before she could be seen. She quietly closed her bedroom door and attempted to eavesdrop on the conversation that took place below.

Her father opened the door to welcome the Andersons, and offered them both something cool to drink as he guided them into the parlor. Ruby eased her way down the stairs slowly to avoid being noticed. She strained to hear the muffled sounds of their conversation and soon detected the faint, sweet smell of her father's pipe tobacco. *Papa must be talking business,* she thought. He often said that smoking his pipe helped him concentrate when he had a lot of thinking to do.

Even though Ruby couldn't make out all that was being said, she knew full well it had something to do with her and Arnold. After an hour of sitting on the stairs, Ruby's eyes were getting tired and had almost closed. Suddenly, she was jarred awake by the sound of footsteps. They were her father's footsteps, and she heard him tell the Andersons, "I'm going to go upstairs to talk to her, but you have nothing to worry about."

By the time he turned the corner, Ruby had managed to dart into her bedroom, jump into bed, and pretend as though she had been reading a book all the while.

Ruby's heart was pounding as she struggled to catch her breath. There was a knock on her door. "Ruby, may I come in and talk with you?" her father asked softly.

She took a deep breath before answering. "Yes, Papa, you can come in." Her tone was reserved, for fear of getting caught spying.

As her father came into her room, she could tell by the look on his face he didn't want to be there any more than she did. But there was no way to avoid each other any longer, or what needed to be done. Now it was his turn to take a deep breath before speaking. "Alfred and Christina Anderson are here, and we've been talking about you and Arnold. But before they leave I told them I needed to talk to you and make sure you can do what's requested of you."

Ruby placed the book on her lap and held onto it like it was the anchor of a ship; something that would keep her strong and steady as the storm slowly approached her. She remained on her bed, sitting in silence with her eyes fixed on her father, waiting for her fate to be announced.

Her father paced back and forth for a moment, searching for the words that would cause the least amount of argument. "Ruby, you know I love you and I only want what's best for you. Just like the Andersons love their son and only want the best for him. Both of us believe that what we've come up with is in the best interest of both families. Me and the Andersons know that you two will learn to love each other in time, but before he leaves for the war you've got to spend time with the boy, and show him what a good wife you'll be to him. When he's in France you must write him often and keep his spirits up."

Her father stopped talking for a moment and waited for a response from his daughter. Ruby was silently looking down at her hands, which were clenched to either side of the book on her lap. Her voice was lost because of the tightness in her throat. She could only manage a whispery, "Yes, Papa."

Her father continued, "I talked to the Andersons, and they agreed the wedding can wait until Arnold, God willing, comes home from the war. You should be pleased with that, I hope. They weren't very happy about it, but I told them that's just how it's got to be."

He saw the relieved look on Ruby's face. "Oh, thank you, Papa!"

But before she could get too carried way with excitement, he told her the last condition of the agreement. "Ruby, if you cannot fulfill your obligation of marriage when Arnold returns home, for any reason, you will be required to find other living arrangements, away from me, your friends, and Amherst."

Ruby's emotions were at odds as she acknowledged the final condition of the agreement. "Yes, Papa, I understand."

Before her father left Ruby's bedroom, he turned to address her one last time. "Ruby, I love you. If you give Arnold a chance I know he'll love you just as much as I loved your mother."

THIRTY-EIGHT

True to the arrangement made by both families, Ruby and Arnold started spending more time together in the following weeks. Two weeks before he was to report for training, Arnold asked Ruby to a dance at the Opera House. Their walk to the dance from Ruby's house was slow and methodical. Arnold would occasionally kick a rock or pinecone, and Ruby looked up to smile as if she were interested in what he was doing. The conversation between them was pleasant, but awkward. There was something missing.

Ruby could see the concerned look in Arnold's eyes when he stopped walking and asked, "Do you suppose there will ever be a day you when you'll love me as much as Ella?"

She was shocked by the question and stopped mid-step. "What in the world are you talking about, Arnold? Where did you ever get such a crazy notion?" Although she tried to pretend his question was foolish, inside her heart was pounding as hard as a locomotive engine.

With a knowing smile Arnold answered, "Ruby, you know how small towns are. People talk. Most of the time talk around here ain't about nothing at all, but sometimes you just need to know the right people to listen to."

Ruby was still stunned by Arnold's question, and started walking quickly toward the Opera House, hoping to avoid talking about it further. All the while, her thoughts raced: should she continue trying to dispel the rumors about her and Ella, or release herself with the truth?

Arnold hadn't intended to upset Ruby, but that's exactly what he had done. He stood hesitantly for a moment, watching Ruby striding ahead, then shouted out, "Ruby, please stop!"

There was no stopping her. She started running as fast as she could toward the Opera House, hoping to find some of her friends there. She could hear Arnold running behind her, begging her to stop.

"Please, Ruby, please stop, will you? Just stop for a minute."

Ruby could see the stairs leading to the entrance, but there were no friends in sight. Since there was no way out, she stopped and turned around. "Arnold Anderson, why do you insist on torturing me like this? Isn't it enough I'm to be your wife when you return from the war?"

"I'm sorry, Ruby, I didn't mean to upset you. But since we're both in this together I thought it best to talk with you about it. I'm sorry. I didn't do a very good job of it. I promise I'll do better. I've never had a girlfriend before, let alone a fiancée. I was only trying to tell you that I understand what you're going though. That's because, well, I'm—"

At that moment Ralph Mathieson, the local bandleader and 'tickled fellow' from Cora's parties, walked up to Ruby and Arnold, as jolly as could be.

"Say, are you two ready to do some dancing tonight?" Then Ralph seemed to sense he was interrupting a serious conversation between Ruby and Arnold and quickly excused himself. But before he did he said, "I hope you two lovebirds aren't having a disagreement." With a wink of his eye and a tip of his hat toward Arnold, he made his way to the Opera House.

Suddenly things started to make sense to Ruby. If Arnold was friends with Ralph, he could have told Arnold about her and Ella. And, if he and Ralph were friends, then maybe she and Arnold had more in common than she could have imagined.

Arnold could tell by the look on Ruby's face that she had made the connection between him and Ralph. "You see, Ruby. I didn't know how to tell you—I understand how you feel, because I feel the same way about Ralph, and I'm just as confused about what to do as you are. But we don't have a choice in the matter. We must start a new life with each other, and start a family. That's what's supposed to happen. Don't you understand, Ruby, that if we don't people will talk, and horrible things could happen to us? I can't imagine what my parents would do if they started hearing some of the gossip."

"Arnold, how will this possibly work for us? Neither of us feel the way a husband and wife should feel about each other. What kind of life will that be for us or our children?"

"I don't know, Ruby, but we must try. Your father said he would get me a good job as the head dairy-hand on a farm in Minneapolis when I return from the war. The day we get married, we must leave this place and all the people we know behind. That's just the way it's going to be."

Unbeknownst to Ruby, that was another part of the marriage agreement. Both families insisted that Arnold and Ruby leave town immediately to start their new life, away from the 'unsavory' people they had associated with in the last few years. Peter Peterson promised the Andersons that he would find Arnold a good job so he could adequately support Ruby and his family.

THIRTY-NINE

After a fifteen-day voyage, Arnold and the other doughboys arrived in France on June 13, 1918. The conditions onboard were cramped and most men suffered from seasickness. However, Arnold questioned the origin of his sickness on the trip in one of his first letters to Ruby. In it he complained about the horrible British food served onboard, and expressed his suspicion that it was likely the cause of the stomach ailments he and his fellow solders suffered from. In the same letter he also pledged that if he were fortunate enough to escape injury while he was there, his sea voyage home would be his last. Needless to say, he and the other men were more than happy to step on solid ground again, even if that meant it was time to fight the Germans.

Arnold belonged to the 81st Infantry Division, also known as the 'Wildcats.' When the Wildcats arrived in Europe they received additional training in trench warfare and were deployed to the Vosges Mountains in France. At the time it was considered a 'quiet front,' although they fought off numerous German raids and artillery bombardments during their assignment.

On the morning of November 11, 1918, the Wildcats planned a pre-dawn attack on a German trench line just north of Bois de Manheulles. Sleep the night before was difficult, because this was the first time his unit was to have direct engagement with the enemy. The fog was thick in the early morning light; Arnold and the other men could barely see two feet in front of them. About a half a mile from there, they were to rendezvous with other solders. The popping sound of machine-gun fire could be heard in the distance. There were screams from some of the men ahead of him, who had become entangled in barbed wire that ran along the trench. Then suddenly his captain shouted out, "Take cover!"

Wet with nervous sweat, the men could hear commands being barked out in German mere feet from where they were, and sound of bullets whizzing overhead. The Wildcats were pinned down by the enemy just along a ridge next to the open trench. At 11:00 a.m. the firing abruptly stopped, but they held their position, waiting for their next command.

It had been thirty minutes, and still there was no sight or sound of the enemy. The captain stretched his neck far enough over the mound of damp dirt to see that the noon sun had burned off the remaining fog, and the hillsides around them were clearly visible. An eerie calm settled into the forest. The captain looked at his men and said in a slow, controlled tone, "It's time to move."

Water quickly filled their boot prints as they walked the open trench, ready to take aim at the first German they saw. Voices could be heard less than a hundred feet away in the dense woods; it wasn't clear if they were friend or foe. They moved cautiously toward the voices, which were beginning to sound more like cheers of joy than screams of war. *Are they American cheers? Have we secured the front line so soon?* Arnold wondered.

Before stepping into the clearing, the men saw American and French soldiers jumping up and down and screaming for joy. A couple of them even did the unthinkable, and fired their rifles into the sky in celebration. The Wildcats slowly walked out of the forest and stood in confusion until a soldier shouted out, "We won! We won! The war is over. We won!"

The Wildcats had only a few hours to celebrate victory over the Germans before starting a 175-mile march back to the nearest rest area.

On that day World War I ended, without Arnold ever having to fire a single shot toward the enemy. However, a new battle would soon begin.

FORTY

With Germany retreating from France, the newspapers were filled with speculation that the war was nearly over. Everyone was overjoyed by this news, except for Ruby. She knew what was expected of her once Arnold returned.

On November 12, 1918, the headlines in the morning papers confirmed Ruby's worst fear: the war was over and victory was officially declared over Germany. She had hoped that Arnold's deployment would linger for many years, rather than only a few months. She knew that she would soon receive a letter from him telling her of his return home. *What will become of me then?* she thought.

Ruby sat in her mother's chair once again for comfort, knowing that no words of solace would come her way. She was alone as she watched the brown fall leaves swirling and turning in the chilly northern wind, becoming entranced by them as they danced across the street. Ruby imagined herself as one of those fallen leaves, being bounced around uncontrollably by invisible forces. She looked on as the brown and brittle leaves tumbled around on the ground—so easily they fractured and then broke, chipping apart into smaller and smaller pieces, until they looked like ordinary grains of dirt on the ground. It was hard to believe that something so strong could become so weak.

Ruby shot up from the chair and started nervously pacing the living room floor, talking to herself. "How in the world will I break the news to Ella and the rest of the ladies and chums? I know Ella is going to be so very upset with me."

She had yet to tell Ella of the marriage arrangements with Arnold— not to deceive her, but because she'd thought she would have years to deliver such news, if at all. Within that much time, she'd allowed herself to imagine that anything could happen. She could decide to leave with Ella for Portland, or Arnold could fall in love with someone in France and choose to stay there. *Wouldn't that be grand?* she thought. But now her dreams were shattered like the broken leaves in the street. Instead of years, she had only months.

With every passing minute Ruby knew her time to marry Arnold was growing nearer, and she felt herself slipping into darkness. How would she ever survive such a life? A life without love and laughter? A life without Ella, girlfriends, and chums? She tried to convince herself that she would be fine, and that her new life with Arnold would be enough. But deep down, she knew it never would be.

FORTY-ONE

Looking past her front yard Ruby could see people running by. *No doubt heading downtown to celebrate victory,* she thought. Just as she started to return to her mother's chair for solace, she stopped, with an idea. *If I can find a job in town before Arnold returns, Papa and the others will have nothing to say about how I live my life.* With that thought, Ruby ran to her room and proceeded to put on her best dress and shoes: the ones she saved for special occasions. She was determined to take control of her life before Arnold returned home to claim her.

She looked at herself in the three-way folding mirror on the dressing table. With one last glance, she was satisfied that her hair and dress were suitable for the business at hand. On the dresser was the last bottle of her mother's rosewater perfume. Ruby removed the cork from the decorative bottle slowly to ensure that not one drop would go to waste. As soon as she smelled the fragrance, thoughts of her mother came pouring in. Being that her mother was a strong independent woman, Ruby was certain she would approve of what she was about to do. She sparingly placed a drop of rosewater perfume behind each ear and on each wrist before walking out the front door. Ruby was off to find a job.

With a determined stride she made her way downtown, past the rush of people heading to the big victory celebration. She entered each store and business with confidence, claiming qualifications she didn't have. The results were all the same. No one was looking to hire.

Her confidence was waning, but she had one last stop to make. She knew Mrs. Wells at the dress shop had no need to hire anyone, but it was her last chance. Since she'd moved to town, Mrs. Wells had become a mother figure for Ruby. Even if there was no work to be done, her words of encouragement were desperately needed.

Mrs. Wells greeted her when she entered the dress store. "Well, Ruby, don't you look real nice today. Are you all dressed up for the victory party tonight?"

With a look of despair Ruby glanced down at her dress. "No. I have no intention of going to the party tonight."

Mrs. Wells could tell by the look on Ruby's face that it had been a difficult day, which seemed odd to her because everyone else was rejoicing over the end of the war. "What's wrong with you, child? You should be heading down to the Opera House, celebrating our victory. The whole town will be there tonight. Maybe you'll be in better spirits by then."

Ruby shot back, "I have no intention of going tonight, because I have no reason to celebrate."

Mrs. Wells was shocked by Ruby's response, but she knew there had to be a reason Ruby was acting the way she was. "Dear girl, what in heaven's name has you so upset?"

"I'm sorry, Mrs. Wells, I shouldn't have said that. It's just that I've gone to every place in town looking for a job today, and no one will hire me. I've done bookkeeping for my father and managed the house and farm for years. What will I do without a job?"

Mrs. Wells was still confused. "Well, Arnold will be home soon. Won't he be able to take care of you?"

Ruby was incensed that everyone in town knew about her impending marriage to Arnold. She even considered that a possible reason why no one wanted to hire her. *They must all expect I'll be starting a family with Arnold soon. I'll never be hired*, she thought.

Ruby looked down at the floor, trying not to burst into tears.

"I don't suppose you've checked with the telephone company already, have you?" Mrs. Wells asked carefully.

Ruby looked up. "The telephone company? They never have any openings. I didn't even consider going there, because I certainly would have heard about it if they were hiring."

Mrs. Wells smiled. "Did you know the Davis family is moving to Chicago in a couple of weeks?"

"I heard about that, but...?" Ruby wasn't sure what Mrs. Wells was getting at.

Mrs. Wells smiled again. "Did you know that their daughter Susan is moving there with them?"

"So?" Ruby replied.

"Susan is a telephone girl, and she'll be leaving her job within ten days." Mrs. Wells gave Ruby a hopeful look and asked, "Do you know how to answer a telephone and talk into it?"

Suddenly, Ruby realized what Mrs. Wells was trying to tell her. Her face lit up, and she leaped over the counter to give her mother-figure a kiss on the cheek. "Of course I do, Mrs. Wells. We have a telephone at home, and Papa tells me all the time I should work for the telephone company because I'm always talking to my friends on it."

Mrs. Wells was pleased to see Ruby back in good spirits. "There's the smile I like to see. Now you go over to the telephone company right now and tell Ed Nelson that I sent you. And that if he ever wants me to tailor his jackets again, he better give you that job."

Ruby was already halfway to the door. "Yes ma'am, I'll do that right now."

There was a hopeful sense of urgency to Ruby's stride as she made her way to the telephone company before everyone in the building left to join the party. As she reached the top of the stairs to the office, she saw

Ed Nelson standing by his desk, putting on his jacket to leave for the day. Before opening the door, she took a deep breath to calm herself and wiped the beads of sweat from her forehead.

Mr. Nelson looked up to see who had entered but continued buttoning his jacket to leave. "Hello, Ruby. The office is closed. You'll have to come back tomorrow."

Ruby knew she had to talk fast. "Mr. Nelson, I'm sorry to interrupt you, but I had to come over and find out if you're looking to hire someone to replace Susan Davis. I understand she's leaving soon and I'm sure I can do her job. We have a telephone at home, and Papa always tells me I should be working for you. I can do your bookkeeping, too."

Mr. Nelson was eager to leave for the evening, and put up his hands to stop her speech. "Ruby, I'm already late for dinner. This will have to wait."

Ruby persisted. "Mrs. Wells told me to come here and talk with you about a job tonight."

He raised his eyebrow. "She did, did she?"

"Yes, Mr. Nelson. She knew I'd be perfect for the job, and she told me I needed to talk with you right away."

Given the look of determination in Ruby's eyes Mr. Nelson knew there was only one way of getting her out of his office. "Ruby, we all know here at the telephone company you can talk on the phone with the best of them. But can you show up on time and never be absent?"

"Yes sir, Mr. Nelson, I most certainly can. You will never have to worry about that with me."

"Very well then, I'll hire you. Come back next Monday to start training. But listen to me, Ruby Peterson, the first time you're late or out sick you'll find yourself out of a job. Now, will you please let me go home before my wife has my hide?"

"Mr. Nelson, I won't let you down. Thank you, Mr. Nelson!"

Ruby now had a reason to celebrate with the rest of the town. She skipped her way over to the Opera House across the street. It was a grand celebration. Ralph was there with his band, of course, to lead people in song and revel in their victory over the Germans. Ruby celebrated her new job and financial independence instead.

FORTY-TWO

June 6, 2015

About fifty minutes into my flight from Los Angeles to Minneapolis, I looked out the window and saw the sandy Red Rock Canyon below. It was a familiar stretch of land I had traveled often when visiting my family in Pahrump, Nevada. I looked farther to the left and saw the outline of Pahrump, the little town where my mother and father lived and are now both buried. It was so strange to be flying thousands of feet over the two people who gave me life. Although I knew the distance was too great, I strained my eyes to try to find the cemetery. No such luck. Oh, how I wished I could tell them about the amazing adventure I was on. I sensed them with me on my journey just the same.

I closed my eyes, knowing that once I arrived in Minneapolis there was still a three-and-a-half-hour drive to Amherst ahead of me. I was startled awake by turbulence and the feeling of the plane descending. I panicked, thinking something must be wrong. My watch indicated there was another fifty minutes until our arrival time. Within moments, the captain announced that because of a strong tailwind we would be arriving much earlier than scheduled.

Minneapolis had never been on my list of places to visit, but there it was. I knew that it was surrounded by lakes—a lot of them—but everything else I knew about the city I learned from watching the *Mary Tyler*

Moore TV show in the 70s. As corny as it sounds, the show's theme song started playing in my head on the final approach for landing.

The show and its theme song were based on a single women's independence and her ability to 'make it on her own' in the big city of Minneapolis.

How appropriate, I thought, as the jet made its final approach to land.

FORTY-THREE

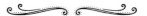

2015

Excited about being on the road and returning to Amherst, the three-and-a-half-hour drive from the airport went quickly as I passed one farm and barn after another. Although this time I was driving from Minneapolis instead of Chicago, the rolling hills of farmland were equally beautiful.

I had a different feeling on my second trip to Amherst. My initial visit was filled with wonder and excitement, because I was seeing everything for the first time. The excitement on this trip came from the feeling in my bones that told me I was returning home.

I pulled up to the Amherst Inn and Bob and Tom were there to greet me. When I walked into the Victorian home the same smell of antique furniture and smoky wood charged my senses. Suitcases in hand, I made my way to the same room I'd stayed in on my first trip. The familiar creaking of the hardwood floor in the hallway seemed to welcome me back.

After unpacking, I lay on the bed to relax after the long drive, and waited for it. It didn't take long before I could hear the rumbling making its way through town; it would be directly behind the inn shortly. The sound that initially frightened me on my first trip was something I now yearned for.

As the roar became louder, I hurried to the open window in my room. I could feel the pounding of the large engine getting closer as it pulled its heavy cargo toward me. I was exhilarated by the roaring sound of metal on metal bursting through the tranquil setting. The room started shaking as if a 5.0-magnitude earthquake was beginning. I watched the massive train pass behind the backyard of the property. The crescendo of the roaring engine gave way to the creaking and groaning of graffiti-covered containers being pulled to an unknown destination.

Then there was silence; the world around me held its breath until it was safe to exhale. Once the train was gone, the backyard returned to the sounds of birds chirping and the trickling of water from the koi pond outside my window.

At night the trains traveled much faster, so the sound was totally different. Their increased speed on the tracks produced a rhythmic melody, much like playing a vinyl record backward. Within the cacophony of sounds, I swear sometimes it sounded as if someone was humming or talking.

This transformation occurred numerous times throughout the day and night, and it was one I never grew tired of or annoyed with. I tried to record the sound of the train, but there was no way to truly capture the thunderous drumming of the engines or hear the beautiful silence after it passed.

After a good night's rest, I woke up early the next morning to start my daily list of things to do. The first thing was to find and visit the home that my great-grandfather, Peter, had purchased in 1916. On my first trip I hadn't realized that he and my grandmother had lived anywhere other than the farm by Lime Lake. However, a month before this trip, I discovered census records with a different address, and on one of my grandmother's photos she had printed 'Our home.' The house was clearly not the same farmhouse I'd seen in the other photos. So a new search had begun.

Prior to my visit I sent photos and census records to Bob and Tom at the inn, and they assured me they knew which home it was. After breakfast I was eager for them to show me where they believed my grandmother lived in 1916. I asked if they wanted me to drive, but they smiled at each other and insisted that wouldn't be necessary. We started walking down Lincoln Street, which was the same side street the inn was located on. As we walked, I noticed how old all of the houses were, and imagined that the street looked much the same as when my Grandma Ruby lived there.

We walked under the railroad bridge located behind the inn. Even though the sign said it had been built in 1913, it was still being used. I could see a hundred years' worth of soot from the trains and cars that traveled over it. There were rust stains on the walls from the metal tracks above and stress cracks from so many years of service. No doubt my grandma would have walked under this same bridge to get to Main Street.

After a five-minute walk, they stopped to show me the home. I couldn't believe how close it was to where I was staying. I had driven past this house many times before on my last trip, with no idea it was another part of the puzzle. My journey was filled with a lot of surprises along the way. It seemed that facts about my grandmother's life were not revealed to me until they were ready to be discovered, or until I was ready to receive them; maybe a little of both.

I quickly confirmed the location by comparing the crescent-shaped window on the front of the house with my grandmother's photo. Then all I could do was stand there and smile as I felt my family greeting me from the front door.

I loved my walks around Amherst, on the same side streets my grandmother walked. Some of the old storefronts were boarded up, but others had been converted into trendy coffee shops, restaurants, or boutiques. The old Opera House still stood, a sturdy brick structure from yesteryear that was abandoned decades ago. Even the wood used to board up the large half-moon entrance and windows was showing signs of wear from the harsh Wisconsin winters.

There was talk about the town's historical society buying the building and having it restored someday. How grand it would be to once again have music and laughter filling the walls and pouring into the streets. I felt my grandmother's spirit stirring in me.

Peterson Home in 1916   *The same home in 2015*

FORTY-FOUR

June 8, 2015

The One-Hundred-Year Anniversary

I woke up that morning with butterflies in my stomach and an eagerness to be where the wedding ceremony of Grandma Ruby and Ella took place. I lay in bed thinking that so much had changed in the last one hundred years. Any day now, the U.S. Supreme Court was to announce its final ruling on marriage equality for same-sex couples in the United States of America. Wow! Did Grandma Ruby, Ella, Cora or the others ever imagine such a thing happening?

The newspaper headlines and stories from a hundred years ago never mentioned LGBTQ people or their issues. That's not because we weren't there. In fact, we, the LGBTQ community, have always been here. We were required to lead invisible lives out of necessity. We loved who we loved in the background of society because it was too dangerous to do otherwise. I hope that future generations never forget or take for granted the equality that so many people before could only dream about, if they dared. I hope they remember the people who fought and died to make the dream of marriage equality a reality.

The sounds of another train approaching took me out of my thoughts. After it passed, I made my way to the kitchen for some coffee.

I was almost too excited to eat, but after seeing Tom's eggs Benedict with homemade hollandaise sauce and hash browns, there was no way for me to pass that up. Tom and Bob knew why I was there and how special the day was to me. It was special to them, too. Since my last visit with them, Tom and Bob had finally been able to get legally married in Wisconsin, on December 21, 2014. After being together for over twenty years, they knew all too well what it felt like to finally have their love and marriage recognized by family, friends, community, and the state they lived in. We were all anxiously awaiting the U.S. Supreme Court's decision to make marriage for LGBTQ people legal across the country.

FORTY-FIVE

June 8, 2015

A couple of months before visiting the Lime Lake farm where Grandma's wedding took place, I sent a letter to Dorothy and her family letting them know about my next visit. I didn't want to make a habit of showing up at Dorothy's doorstep unannounced. In my letter, I explained why I wanted to come. However, I didn't indicate who the people in the wedding were. I guess a part of me was afraid of rejection if they found out how special the ceremony really was. I never heard back from Dorothy or her family telling me they opposed my visit, so I took that as a good sign.

I was nervous as I turned onto the private road leading to their property. I drove slowly and put my phone on video mode. On my last trip the trees and meadows had still been brown from the harsh winter, but this time there was an explosion of greenery on the hillside, with flowers in bloom and tree limbs so full of leaves they draped the road like giant umbrellas.

The shady tree-lined road led me to the home and property that I'd studied for years. I had memorized the hillside, the house, and the barn from my last trip. Everything, except for the spring season, looked exactly the same. As I pulled up to the home, I could see a woman walking near the side of the house. I hardly had time to turn off the engine before being greeted by Dorothy's daughter. I held out my hand to introduce myself, but her smile told me she already knew who I was. I'm sure she was there to make sure her mother was looked after. I would do the same thing if some stranger from Los Angeles was writing letters and visiting my mother.

I asked how her mother was, and as if on cue, Dorothy opened the kitchen door leading to the backyard driveway. I was happy to see her. After all, I know how fragile life can become when a person is in her nineties. She seemed to be just as full of life as when I met her a year earlier. We talked for a moment, and then she asked me if I'd like to see the inside of the house. Of course I wanted to, but I never wanted to intrude that way. Up to that point I could only use my imagination to envision what it looked like inside.

My breath was heavy with excitement as I walked into the house. Even with the renovations, sections of the original house were still visible. The house felt very much like home to me. When I first stepped inside, it was smaller and darker than I thought it would be. In the living room to my left there was hardly enough room for a couch and two armchairs. The kitchen to my right was much larger and brighter, and I could tell it had been expanded with the renovation. When I complimented Dorothy on her large kitchen, I could see the pride in her eyes as she told me there had been no running water in the home when she and her husband first moved in. I easily sensed that the kitchen was the heart of their home.

Then Dorothy started showing me her old family photos, displayed on the living room walls. Her eyes sparkled as she showed me her wedding photos and pictures of her kids. As Dorothy spoke to me, I tried hard to concentrate, but my mind was going in a thousand different directions. I couldn't get over the fact that I was standing in the house where my grandmother Ruby had lived—the home of my great-grandparents, and the place my Great-Grandmother Hilda died in 1912. I stood there for a moment, taking it all in. Between my family and Dorothy's, there were so many memories held in the walls of this sweet old home.

About fifteen minutes had gone by and I could feel the outside pulling at me. It had something to show me. As I made my way to the door,

I thanked Dorothy and her daughter for sharing their home and family with me. Like the last time I was there, I asked if I could walk around the property and take photos. They both graciously agreed. There are not many places nowadays where people will allow a stranger to walk into their home—at least none that I know of. Or maybe I've just become too hardened by city life.

Stepping outside, I heard the faint sound of metal wind chimes being pushed by the spring breeze. The birds in the background chirped in unison, as if discussing what a special day it was. It had rained heavily the day before and I worried it would continue, but the sky was brilliant blue, with only a few cotton-candy clouds hanging over the bright green hillsides.

With a calm sense of serenity I walked the property. I was there to honor my grandmother and her marriage to Ella. Absorbing all the sights and sounds, I thought about the many events and people that had brought me to this place on this date. As I walked to the place where the wedding ceremony had been held, I saw a white plastic bench under one of the trees. Clearly Dorothy took comfort in resting underneath the same trees. The thought of my grandmother and Ella flooded every part of me, and I felt the joy that was felt that day.

I looked up at the same two beautiful elm trees that had provided shade so long ago. Now thick and twisted with age, they stood like tall protectors of the land, proud of the one-hundred-year secret held securely in their roots. I was humbled as I stood underneath the trees where so much love and bravery took place. I often wondered whether or not I would have been as brave as my grandma and the women in her photos, if I'd been born back then. I'd like to think that I would be.

Before walking away, I touched one of the trees and watched an elm seed fluttering in the wind like a broken helicopter. After it hit the ground, I picked it up and held it in my hand. *One last gift from the trees,* I thought as I put the seed into a plastic bag.

I still have that seed. It's a reminder of that day and of the love that happened there so long ago. It also reminds me that sometimes the biggest changes can be made when one small seed is allowed to take root.

June 8, 2015

FORTY-SIX

With the words from Mr. Nelson still ringing in her head about being late, Ruby was on her way to her first day on the job. Even though the walk would take only ten minutes, she left home that cold morning twenty minutes before her starting time. Her steps were quick and purposeful as she reached the top of the stairs. Mr. Nelson was at his desk reading the *Stevens Point Journal,* and was pleased to see Ruby arrive ahead of schedule.

Ruby hadn't yet told her father about her new job as the town telephone girl. She'd intended to do it before he left home for business, but she couldn't find the courage. She knew he would discourage her working, maybe even forbid it, given the fact that Arnold would be returning home sooner than expected. But Ruby figured that if she was already working when her father returned home, there would be little he could do to make her quit.

After her shift was done Friday evening, she walked across the street to the Opera House to visit with friends. She had just been given her first week's wages from Mr. Nelson and could hear the sweet sound of coins jingling in the front pocket of her dress. By the time she reached her friends, she had already thought about how her first bit of real income would be spent. The new yellow dress in Mrs. Wells' shop would be hers by the end of the week.

The sky was dark with winter as she rounded the corner to her home and saw light coming from inside her house. *Papa's home,* she thought. Before opening the front door, Ruby put her hands in her dress pockets to feel the five-and-a-half dollars Mr. Nelson had paid her for the week's work.

The smell of pipe tobacco was heavy and hung in the room like storm clouds. She knew her father was troubled by something. She had a terrible feeling when she saw him sitting at the dinning room table, with rings of smoke curling around his head. She already knew what he was thinking.

Her father grimaced when he saw her, and exhaled a large puff of smoke. "So what's this I hear you're trying to get a job at the telephone company?"

Ruby's fears were confirmed.

"Papa, I tried to tell you before you left, but I didn't know how. Please don't be angry with me. I just wanted to show you and everyone else that I can earn a good living and take care of myself. What's the harm in that?"

"Ruby Peterson, the harm is that your fiancé will be returning home in the next few months and you should be preparing for the wedding, not worrying about finding a job. I will not allow you to work there."

Ruby pulled her hands from her pocket and showed her father her earnings.

"Papa, It's too late. I started working there on Monday and they've already trained me. Mr. Nelson said I'm one of the best telephone girls he's ever had. If I quit now, Mr. Nelson will be horribly upset with me. Once Arnold returns I swear I'll quit. But I don't see any reason why I can't earn a living in the meantime."

Although Ruby's father was still upset, he was a man of reason. As long as Ruby agreed to quit when Arnold returned, he would allow her to work as the town telephone girl. "All right then," he told her. "But don't think for a minute that you're gonna get out of marrying that boy. I've already told the entire family about the wedding and I'm sure the Andersons have done the same. None of us want to be embarrassed because of you."

Even though Ruby agreed with her father, that didn't mean that something couldn't change by the time Arnold got home. She prayed something would.

With the disgruntled approval of her father, Ruby continued her job as the telephone girl. A bonus of Ruby's job was that Cora and the gals now had an inside liaison to communicate events and parties. As she became more proficient with the complicated switchboard, she also became the point person for any upcoming event within and around town. Also, with Ruby working the switchboard, there was less concern about being eavesdropped on by nosy people who might report any 'deviant' romantic conversations to Mr. Nelson or the authorities. Things couldn't have been better if they'd planned it that way.

Still, Ruby's troubles weighed heavily on her mind. She wondered when Arnold would return, and what she would do when he did. Her last letter from Arnold indicated that he might not be home for another eight months. Even though the war was over, the Wildcats were still needed to guard bridges and other important locations while the French were busy rebuilding their cities and towns.

Her other concern was what to tell Ella, and how. She hadn't seen Ella in several months, and still had yet to disclose the marriage arrangements with Arnold. Even with full telephone access, having that conversation with Ella over the phone seemed impossible. Regardless of how the news was delivered, she feared Ella would have nothing more to do with her, and any thoughts of moving to Portland would be quickly dispelled. But she knew the deed must be done.

FORTY-SEVEN

April 1919

Ella had made plans to visit Ruby over Easter weekend. Ruby was happy about the visit, but dreaded the outcome. Ella was aware Ruby had to work that weekend, and rented a room at the hotel next to the telephone company. Ella rather enjoyed the idea of greeting Ruby with a warm bath after her shift ended. To Ella, there was nothing more alluring than two strong, independent women enjoying each other's company.

By the time Ella arrived that Saturday afternoon, Ruby was exhausted. She had just worked seven days straight, and the last two days were double shifts. Mr. Nelson expected her to work the following day as well. Their reunion was warm, but Ella could tell Ruby was about to fall over with fatigue. After Ruby finished her bath, Ella wrapped towels around her, kissed her forehead, and led her to bed.

Ella watched Ruby as she quickly fell asleep and wondered what would become of them both. She was proud of Ruby for taking her job so seriously, and hoped that was a good sign of her independence. Ella knew the pressure Ruby was under to get married and wondered if she had the strength and independence needed to move to Portland with her. Before falling asleep, Ella prayed that this time her love would win, and by the coming fall they would be moving to the West Coast.

That next morning Ruby woke up to the sunlight streaming through the hotel room's stained-glass windows and tapestry curtains. Still half-asleep, Ruby watched Ella sitting at the writing table grading test papers. Ella was facing the wall, her hair haphazardly pinned up into a bun on the back of her head. A few waves of dark hair broke free and flowed with the curve of her neck. Ruby was content watching in silence as Ella read each paper, occasionally nodding in acknowledgement of a job well done by a student. Her contentment took Ruby back to the week they got married. Then her heart started beating faster, wondering what would become of them once she broke the news about Arnold.

Even with Ella's back facing the bed, she sensed that Ruby was awake. She smiled and turned around. "There you are. I was afraid you might sleep all day."

Ruby bolted up from bed. "Oh my God! What time is it?"

Ella laughed. "Relax, it's only eight o'clock. You told me last night you didn't go into work today until eleven. I wouldn't dare let you oversleep."

Ruby eased her way back into bed and waited to catch her breath. Watching Ella sitting at the desk excited her. So much so that she forgot about the dreaded information she needed to share—instead, passion was calling her. "So, are you going to be grading homework all day?" she asked with a smile.

Ella felt electricity running up her spine and was quick to respond, "How am I expected to work with a beautiful woman in my bed?"

Ruby pulled back the covers to welcome Ella back to bed. "I've got to be at work in three hours."

FORTY-EIGHT

It was ten o'clock, and Ruby was getting ready for her eleven o'clock shift. Ella had gone down to the restaurant to get them both a cup of coffee. Ruby knew what had to be done. She had to tell Ella about the wedding arrangements with Arnold.

When Ella returned, Ruby reached for her hand and led her toward the bed without saying a word.

At first Ella smiled and said, "Now Ruby, you don't want to be late for work, do you?" Then she noticed Ruby had a serious look on her face that told her romance was not on Ruby's mind.

"No, Ella. I need to tell you something."

Ella was caught off-guard after the love they'd shared that morning. She was concerned about what Ruby had to tell her, but figured that whatever it was, they would be fine.

They sat next to each other on the side of the bed. The room was filled with a heavy silence, as Ruby searched for the words she knew would change everything.

Ella's stomach tightened as the silence continued to fill the room, until she could take no more. "Ruby, you're frightening me. What is it? What's wrong?"

Ruby covered her eyes with her hands as the tears began to fall. "Ella, I don't know how to tell you this. I swear I don't."

Ella braced herself by putting her hand on Ruby's shoulder. "Ruby, just calm down and tell me what's going on."

With her hands still covering her eyes, Ruby said to Ella, "My father and the Andersons want me to marry their son, Arnold, when he returns from France."

The weight of Ella's hand fell from Ruby's shoulder. "What are you telling me, Ruby? Are you telling me you want to marry him?"

"No, Ella! I don't want to marry him. I'm already married. Remember? That's why I got this job, so my father and my family could see that I can take care of myself, that I don't need a man to take care of me. I thought he would be gone for a few years. God help me, I even hoped he wouldn't come back at all. But now that the war is over he'll likely be home by the end of the year."

Ella was confused. "So did you tell your father and the Andersons that you won't be marrying him when he returns?"

Ruby sat in silence, still unable to look at her.

Ella's heart fell to a horribly familiar place. The same place it had been five years ago when Alice left her to marry a man, a man who was also chosen by her parents. Tears formed in Ella's eyes. She hated crying. She prided herself on shedding so few tears in her life, but for this there was no way to hide her emotions.

Ruby tried to comfort Ella by telling her, "Ella, please listen to me. I had to agree to the arrangements. I was afraid Papa was going to kick me out of the house. Then what would I do?"

Ella shot back, "You can leave with me now. We can start our own life together now. How horrible would that be?"

"It's not that easy, Ella. I would be leaving my family. I'd likely never see my brothers and sisters ever again. My father would hate me, and he'd hate himself, thinking he had failed. That's why I agreed to the

DON'T YOU DARE

marriage—but I don't intend to go through with it. I just need more time to figure things out."

Ella's world was spinning out of control. It felt as if the air inside the room was too thin to breathe. She stood up without saying a word and started packing her bags. She had to leave; she could bear no more.

Ruby was still sitting on the bed, watching Ella pack. "Please don't go, Ella. I love you. If you love me, please don't go."

Ella turned to face Ruby with anger and heartbreak in her eyes. "Ruby, you know I love you. If you really loved me, you would never ask me to stay and watch you marry someone else. I've been made a fool of for the last time. It is very simple. You can either move with me to Portland, or you can stay here and live a miserable life with Arnold and your family. But I will not wait in the background."

With two hearts broken, Ella motored back home to Sheboygan and Ruby went to work. However, with all the commotion that morning, Ruby didn't realize she was almost twenty minutes late for work. It did not go unnoticed by Mr. Nelson.

Ruby was so distraught after Ella left that she wasn't sure how she would finish her shift. She kept on replaying their conversation over in her head. She was brought back to reality by the sounds of the switchboard buzzing from multiple phone calls waiting to be connected. Her head was pounding, and the sound was amplified through the ringing in her ears. All the lights on the switchboard were lit up, and buzzers were going off in unison. The cables and wires leading into the switchboard looked like a giant monster, ready to attack her. She haphazardly connected the calls until the noise stopped. Relieved by the return of silence, she recalled Ella crying and how hopeless she looked packing her bags before leaving.

Mr. Nelson stormed into the switchboard room.

"Ruby, what in the blazes is going on in here? Mrs. Olson just came into the office complaining that she's been trying to call the doctor all afternoon because her husband is ill and you keep connecting her to the mortician."

Ruby could instantly see her boss was upset. "I'm sorry, Mr. Nelson. I've got a horrible headache. I'm not feeling well. I'll do better, please just let me finish my shift."

Mr. Nelson had no sympathy for her. "Ruby, you were twenty minutes late today and now I'm receiving complaints that you're not doing your job. I told you when I hired you what would happen. I'll finish your shift today and have a replacement for you tomorrow."

Mr. Nelson took over to regain control of the switchboard as Ruby pleaded her case. "Mr. Nelson, I beg of you. Please give me another chance. This job means everything to me. I swear this will never happen again."

Mr. Nelson was oblivious to Ruby's request for forgiveness and continued to answer the buzzing switchboard.

FORTY-NINE

After losing the one and only real job she'd ever had, the remainder of 1919 wasn't any easier for Ruby. Although she looked for other jobs, she ended up going back to doing bookkeeping for her father. He paid her two dollars a week. *No way to save money at that rate,* she thought.

Ruby wrote to Ella a week after she left, begging for forgiveness and pleading for more time. Even though they both knew time had already run out, they continued corresponding throughout the year.

Ella was resolved that she would not visit Ruby under the circumstances. By the end of summer, she delivered her final ultimatum to Ruby: "I am moving to Portland in six months, and must know by the end of the year what your intentions are, and if you will be joining me."

Ruby was still waiting to hear from Arnold about his return. It was agonizing not knowing when her life would be expected to end. Finally, on October 29, 1919, a letter arrived informing her that Arnold would be home on February 25th of the next year. Once news of Arnold's return got out, locals started planning a celebration party to welcome back one of their hometown heroes from the war. Everyone in town congratulated Ruby on the safe return of her fiancée. Although she smiled and thanked them, she knew that her war had just begun.

Without any means to support herself, Ruby knew there was no way to avoid the inevitable. Leaving with Ella for Portland was an impossible dream. As much as she wanted to go, she couldn't abandon her father, not now. He had taken ill in the last few months and started losing sight in his right eye. She feared leaving would cause him more health problems, or even kill him. If something were to happen to him she would hate herself, and most assuredly be hated by her brothers and sisters.

At Ella's request, Ruby stopped calling her until she decided what she was going to do. They both knew it was for the best, but when Ruby could take no more she would call just to hear Ella's voice. When Ella answered, she could only hear the crackling of the telephone line and a faint whisper of someone weeping before the caller hung up.

"Ruby, is that you? Ruby?" Ella knew who it was, and cried to herself when the phone line went dead. When she fell in love with Ruby, she of course hoped things would be different this time. In her heart, she still prayed Ruby would have the strength to leave with her for the West Coast. She continued to dream about buying a house where they both would live overlooking the salty blue Pacific Ocean.

To occupy her mind, Ruby started going to church every day. She prayed that God would give her strength to do what was expected of her and to find a place for Arnold in her heart. She engulfed herself in a world she had little interest in, and was resigned to the fact that she somehow had to try.

She desperately wanted to go to Cora's parties to feel like her old self again, but feared the forlorn look from the others—the look that said without words how they pitied what her life would become in the next few months. By that time, all of them were aware of what was expected of her when Arnold returned. Cora and the ladies wanted to throw Ruby a going-away linen party, but she refused. She wanted nothing to do with such a party. She was already depressed enough, and didn't want to see the fear and pain in their eyes as well.

Thanksgiving had come and gone, and now winter was taking over the landscape with a light flurry of snow. The snow was too delicate to stick to the ground; it was just enough to warn the last bit of greenery that its time was also near. In a matter of weeks, Ella would be coming home to Almond to visit family for the Christmas holidays. Ruby knew that her time was near as well: Ella was expecting a final answer before the end of the year.

Pen in hand, Ruby started writing a letter to Ella telling her of her final decision. Ruby had had so many years to think about what this moment would look like. She'd always thought when the time came the direction would be clear. But with Arnold returning home soon, it seemed so unfair that she should have to make such a dire decision. *Why can't things just stay the way they are?*

FIFTY

November 20, 1919

When Ella came home for the Christmas holiday, there was a letter waiting for her. The handwriting on the envelope looked shaky, and she could barely tell who it was from. Then she made out the name Peter Peterson, and knew it was from Ruby. Without opening it, she knew the contents would change everything. Would Ruby have the courage to move to the West Coast with her? Would she move away from the small farm-town mentality and gossip, to a place that was more open-minded, and not so damn freezing?

Ella sat on the couch and waited for her hands to stop shaking from the cold. They were also shaking in anticipation of what the letter contained. Before opening it, she put the letter on the table and stared at it for almost twenty minutes. She closed her eyes to pray one last time before taking a breath to open it.

> *My Dearest Ella,*
>
> *I trust you had a safe trip home and you are well. Winter has just started and already I can't wait for it to end. I suppose you want to know if I've decided to move with you to the West Coast. My Darling, in the last six months I have done nothing but think about it, and you ever since. It sounds so wonderful, but I hope you understand that I cannot go with you and leave*

my family behind. I must do what my father has asked of me and marry Arnold when he returns. I know you will be terribly disappointed with my decision, and I can only hope someday you will find a way to forgive me.

By the time you read this I will have traveled to my Uncle and Aunt's home in Milwaukee to spend Christmas Holiday. Please do not come looking for me, I cannot bear to see the disappointment in your eyes.

Your Beloved Always,

Pete

Ruby's letter fell to the floor by the couch. Ella cupped her hands together as if to pray, but she was holding her hands as a way to control her emotions. The feeling of wanting to lash out at something or someone consumed her. As her heart sank into darkness and her vision blurred with tears, she asked herself, *How could my love have deceived me so? How will I recover from a love I will never truly have? Why was my love not enough for her? Why was it so easy for her to walk away from what we had?*

Ella honored Ruby's request and never attempted to see or contact her ever again. She knew Ruby's words were as permanent as the ink they were written with. She also knew that there was no way to cure, change, or fix how she loved. Any attempt to do so would certainly drive her mad.

FIFTY-ONE

After receiving Ruby's letter, Ella tried to convince herself that she hated Ruby for what she had done. But deep down inside, she knew that could never be true. She knew that Ruby would always love her too. What she didn't know was the emotional toll the letter had taken on Ruby.

It had taken her a week to compose the letter, before sending it on the 16th of December. She had written and rewritten it so many times that her fingers had formed blisters from tightly gripping the pen. She would only stop writing to pray. She prayed that God would give her strength to know what to do. Ruby was unable to sleep because of the endless visions of Ella and Cora and the other ladies that appeared when she closed her eyes. She could barely bring herself to eat; it felt as if her throat had become too narrow to swallow.

Ruby's father had noticed the emotional distress his daughter was going through. He knew she wasn't happy about marrying Arnold, but he didn't understand the depth of her emotions. After all, this was what young ladies were expected to do. Since Ruby would be turning twenty-five years old next year, he felt obligated to make sure his daughter did not become an 'old maid.'

Growing more concerned with her behavior, he decided to contact Ada for assistance. When he told Ada how her sister was behaving, she suspected she knew why. Ada knew that Ruby was not like the rest of the family, but she'd figured that when it was time to settle down and get married, Ruby would be able to put her personal feelings aside and do what was required.

When Ada arrived and walked into Ruby's bedroom, she was shocked by her younger sister's appearance.

"Sister! What are you doing here?" Ruby asked.

Ada put her hand on her hips and responded, "Well, you're scaring Daddy half to death because of how you're acting. Look at yourself, Ruby. You look a mess. Your eyes are as dark as two burnt holes in a blanket."

Ruby looked into the mirror next to her bed and saw the dark circles her sister was referring to. Her face was pale and sunken from the lack of food. It didn't look like she had brushed her hair or taken a bath in weeks. After looking at herself in the mirror, she realized her sister was right, and tried to straighten her hair with her hands as best she could.

Unable to contain herself any longer, Ruby fell into her sister's arms and cried. Ada was not used to seeing her sister this way and realized she had underestimated the relationship between her and Ella. As the two held each other, Ruby looked at her sister and asked, "Ada, I know why I'm crying, but why are you?"

Ada wiped away her tears. "I never should have allowed you to get mixed up with Cora and all her friends. I should have stopped you when I saw what was happening between you and Ella. If I had, none of this would be going on. I should have stopped it, but you seemed so happy. I didn't think this would happen. I've made a terrible mess out of things."

Ruby could tell her sister was going to continue, and shouted, "Please stop, Ada!"

Ada stopped and took a step back to look at her sister.

"Ada, you did not cause this mess. Ella, Cora, or any of her friends didn't cause this to happen to me, either. I have always prayed and wished I was like you and everyone else, but I'm not. I don't love Arnold, nor will I ever. I love Ella. I love her the same way any woman loves a man. I suppose you must think I'm a monster, or that I've gone mad, or something like that, but I'm not. Ella and I have been talking about moving to the West Coast. If I go, would you visit me there? Would any of our other brothers or sisters ever visit me there? Would Papa still love me and would he visit me? Please tell me, sister, what shall I do?"

Ada sat on the side of Ruby's bed. "Ruby, you know I love you and would never want anyone or anything to hurt you. But how could you ever live that way? Don't you know what people will say about you and Ella? What kind of life would that be? If you leave, I'm afraid it might kill Papa, and the family would be torn apart. Arnold's a good man, and he'll take good care of you. You two can live somewhere around Stevens Point, and we can see each other whenever we want."

Ruby heard every word Ada told her and knew her sister was right. As much as she loved Ella, the thought of never seeing her family again and breaking her father's heart was too much to bear. She must try to do what was expected of her and marry Arnold Anderson. With a shaking hand, she wrote her final letter to Ella.

The days after she sent the letter to Ella provided no relief for the pain she felt. Ruby locked herself in her bedroom and contemplated doing the worst. She wished that Lime Lake were not already frozen solid, because she would like to walk to her favorite place after sunset and fill her lungs with the sweet dark water as it sparkled in the moonlight.

There was a knock on Ruby's bedroom door. "Ruby, are you ready to go?" Ada asked through the door. "If we're going to be at Aunt Ida's and Uncle Ole's house by supper we need to leave soon."

FIFTY-TWO

In February 1920, Ella was brought before the school board to defend her teachings from the book *Im Vaterland* to her second-year German class. The literal translation of this 416-page book's title is *My Fatherland*. It had been used in German language classrooms throughout the United States since it was first published in 1910. However, with the severed relationship between the U.S. and Germany, the book became highly controversial.

Even though there was no political agenda or message within the book, it was considered by many to be 'anti-American.' The primary objective of the text was to deepen and explain the differences between German and American customs for students who might never travel abroad. The lessons in *Im Vaterland* included German vocabulary, poetry, history, music, and mythology. Unfortunately, it also contained a photo of the hated Kaiser Wilhelm II, on the inside cover.

Ella saw no harm in teaching from this book because it was about her culture, and was far removed from the most recent events taking place in the world. The book also reminded her of her childhood days in eastern Germany, before the darkness of dictatorship and anti-Semitic thought took hold of her beloved country. She hated the Kaiser just as much as any other U.S. citizen, for what he had done to her homeland. However, that did not prevent her from being questioned about her patriotism when others found out about the book.

When the father of one of her students saw the photo of the Kaiser, he brought it to the attention of the local newspaper, the *Sheboygan Press*. A reporter then contacted Mr. Urban, the principal of the school, for a statement. He was furious and vowed to remedy the situation immediately, but it was too late. The next morning he woke up to find the newspaper had already printed the story—on the front page, no less.

A special school board meeting was held that week to discuss the matter of Ella's teaching material. Mr. Urban, Ella, three stuffy board members, and a representative from the *Sheboygan Press* were in attendance.

Mr. Urban was as jumpy as a cat, fearing he would be held responsible for Ella's teaching material. Ella could see that Mr. Urban's white shirt was wet with perspiration under his heavy wool suit, even though it was just as cold inside as it was outside in the snow. The three stoic board members sat quietly. She was sure they already knew what the end result of the meeting would be, but she had to try to salvage as much of her teaching material as she could.

Once the meeting was called to order, Mr. Urban pulled at the collar of his shirt and cleared his throat. He uttered his sincere regret that the book had not been discarded years ago. "It was simply an oversight that the book has been used in the high school for the past eight years. Since the outbreak of the war, all poetry and reading matter lauding Germany has been omitted, as we do everything in our power to stimulate a spirit of patriotism in our student body. The book has been used here for such a long time that the possibility of it containing objectionable matter did not enter my mind until I read the article in the press and people spoke to me about it. Then I immediately took steps to remedy the situation. It is regrettable that my attention was not called to it sooner, as I would never sanction the use of books which might be detrimental to the spirit of patriotism which we are striving to inject and cultivate at all times."

Ella listened quietly to Mr. Urban. *Look at him squirming in his seat like a frightened little boy. They have no idea how beautiful it was there before that damn Kaiser went crazy and turned the world against us. These small-minded men will never allow me to teach my students what the real Germany was like, but I shall try.*

After Mr. Urban delivered his speech, the attention of the board members and press turned toward Ella. She maintained a look of resolve, but she was just as frightened as her principal. She had the same sick feeling in her stomach as the night she had been attacked outside her home four years ago, only this time the attack was in plain sight. Ella knew she had to tread lightly for her own safety, as well as for her teaching career, but she would not let her fear be known.

"Miss Karnopp," said Mr. Urban, "I would like to have you give us some exact information with regard to the use of the supplementary reader, *Im Vaterland*. I understand it has some objectionable material. Just what is that material and how have you handled it?"

Ella replied, "It is true that the picture of Kaiser appears prominently as the frontispiece and that there were some poems and other matter lauding Germany, but since the severing of relations between America and Germany, I do not permit my students to translate or study such material as '*Deutschland, Deutschland Uber Alles*.'[1] The book ought not be used, but my students had invested money in the purchase of it and I did not think it fair to ask them to buy another text. It appeared to me that the most feasible plan was to omit the objectionable parts."

Mr. Urban rebutted Ella's statement. "I agree that no additional expense should be imposed upon the students, Miss Karnopp. Therefore, you must make an effort to find suitable substitute books from the library for *Im Vaterland*. Certainly there is sufficient supply of other supplementary readers in the library for our students to use."

Ella interjected, "None of the latest German supplementary readers are absolutely devoid of unpatriotic material. Practically all of them contain '*Die Wacht Am Rhein*,'[2] the German national song, and other objectionable

1 Translation: "Germany, Germany Above All"
2 Translation: "The Watch on the Rhine"

verse. Book companies are now printing German readers which have no matter that might jeopardize American patriotism, but they have not yet been issued. Whatever book my classes use, I shall be very strict about omitting the objectionable parts."

Mr. Urban was unmoved by Ella's argument. "I order that *Im Vaterland* be immediately removed from this high school building and suggest that your students tear out the picture of the Kaiser before taking the book home. Miss Karnopp, if you are not able to find a suitable replacement for this book, you shall teach from the text *Democracy Today* from our standard English class. This book has a front piece picture of President Woodrow Wilson and is a clear exposition of the ideals of democracy for which the United States is fighting."

With that, Mr. Urban picked up his gavel and slammed it to the desk to enforce his ruling. The sound of the gavel bore a hole into Ella as it echoed in the cold room and traveled down the hallway. But Ella did not flinch or respond at all as she sat in silence in front of the three stuffy school board members. She understood that compromising in teaching was not only prudent for her career: it was needed for her personal safety as well, at least until she found another suitable teaching position.

FIFTY-THREE

Arnold, dressed in his best military uniform, looked down at the handful of U.S. government pamphlets given to him before boarding the train. One congratulated him on winning the war against autocracy, and the other told him what to expect when he returned home—something he'd spent most of his time thinking about on his return trip aboard the U.S.S. Martha Washington. He was returning home from his division in France as a sergeant. This was his last train ride, from Chicago to Amherst, where he'd be greeted as a hometown hero. He rested his eyes, knowing the next part of his mission would be the most difficult to complete.

Arnold's early release from the military had nothing to do with him satisfying his enlistment. It was his father's doing. On April 22, 1919, Alfred Anderson sent a notarized statement to the State Department claiming Arnold was needed back home because of Alfred's failing health. Since Arnold was an only son, he was given an early honorable discharge from military service to assist his father on the farm.

The reason for Arnold's early release was unknown to Ruby, who did her part in keeping his spirits up with weekly letters. The fact that Ruby's letters to him usually addressed him as 'Dearest Friend,' concerned him about her willingness to go through with their wedding.

Arnold woke from his light sleep to a young boy staring at him. "Hello son, what's your name?" he asked.

"My name is James. Did you shoot and kill any of those dirty Germans?"

Arnold was caught off-guard by the youngster's question. "Well, I—I didn't shoot any of them, I'm sorry to tell you."

He could see in James' eyes that his war story was disappointing. "No, I didn't shoot any of them, because I was in charge of the cannons. I blasted hundreds of them out of their bunkers so the other soldiers could kill them."

James' face lit up. "Wow! Really? Mommy, did you hear that? He shot cannons at the Germans."

James' mother was sitting just behind Arnold and came over to collect her inquisitive son. "James! Get over here right now. I'm so sorry, every time he sees a soldier he does this."

Arnold was pleased that his harmless untruth was able to match the young boy's fantasy of war, until James' mother said, "I'm afraid he wants to fight in a war like his father did. My husband was in one of the first regiments that went over there to fight the Germans. But he didn't make it home. I'm so glad that horrible war is over with. I'm sure your family and sweetheart are overjoyed for you to be coming home as well."

The guilt of Arnold's well-intentioned white lie burned in his stomach. He could hardly look at the widowed woman, knowing the only time he'd fired his rifle was at the shooting range. "I'm sorry for your loss, ma'am. I'm sure your husband was a good man."

Tears formed in the woman's eyes. "Yes, he was," she said softly, and then she turned and made her way back to her son.

Arnold was silenced by the woman's confession about losing her husband to war. He looked down at his nicely cleaned uniform and felt the urge to rip it from his body. His gut ached from the acid churning in his stomach, and sweat started running down his forehead. *So many lies,* he thought.

He gazed out the window at the snowy landscape and was unable to recognize his own reflection. He thought, *I look like a man who has fought in a war. I look like a man eager to return home to his family and sweetheart. I look like a man who enjoys the company of a woman's touch. But I am none of those things.*

Soon the rhythmic pulse of the train started to slow. Arnold felt his heart beating faster as the thumping of the tracks came further and further apart. He could see the corner of the train station, and then the platform with almost two dozen people huddled together, no doubt in an effort to keep themselves warm in the freezing January cold.

The train engine delivered a blast of steam to the crowd as it passed. So much steam that, for a split second, it appeared as though the gatherers had disappeared. In that brief moment, Arnold closed his eyes and prayed for it to be true. As the cloud of steam lifted he could see the outline of his mother and father standing in front of the well-wishers.

A man in the crowd spotted Arnold and shouted, "There he is!"

Everyone began waving, and the sound of the song "For He's a Jolly Good Fellow" pushed through the walls and windows of the train. *My good lord, they brought a band too,* he thought, and grimaced.

Arnold stood on the top stair of the train, searching the crowd. He looked to the left to follow the music and saw Ralph leading the band in another round of the popular song. He looked so handsome with his conductor's uniform on. With baton in hand, Ralph looked over his shoulder at Arnold and discreetly gave him one of his famous winks.

Arnold quickly looked away, now desperate to find her—like a drowning man looking for a life preserver. *She must be here,* he thought. He finally spotted her standing just a few feet away from his parents. It was a hopeless moment in time for Arnold. He wanted to run toward Ralph, but knew he had no choice in the matter. Instead, he dropped his bags and ran toward Ruby.

With her hands tucked under her arms to keep warm, Ruby hardly expected what happened next. Onlookers watched Arnold as he picked her up and leaned her back with a kiss. With her legs helplessly dangling off the ground, she wanted to push him away. The crowd erupted into cheers, thinking they were witnessing two lovebirds reunited. However, Arnold and Ruby knew all too well how looks could be deceiving.

FIFTY-FOUR

September 1920

As Ella's train pulled away from the station, she looked at her reflection in the window. She could see in her own eyes how Ruby's final words had destroyed her. Every time she thought about what could have been, her heart fell deeper in her chest. So much so that she wondered if it was possible for it to stop beating altogether. There would be no perfect home overlooking the brilliant blue Pacific Ocean with the woman she loved. Instead, Ella would start her new life alone. She was desperately trying to hold back her tears by reminding herself that, *Men—real men—don't cry.*

The night before, Ella had packed for her long and lonely train ride to Portland. There were many reasons for her to dread the journey: one of them was the scornful looks she expected from fellow passengers because she was traveling alone. A respectable woman would be accompanied by a gentleman.

Ella carefully folded her best gentleman's suit before putting it in her suitcase. She stopped to examine it when she noticed a loose piece of thread on the lapel. That was when all the memories came flooding in. It was the same jacket she'd worn on her wedding day, June 8th—the day she and Ruby pledged their love for each other underneath the shade trees in Ruby's backyard. Ella ran her hand down the right sleeve and recalled how much she'd loved it when Ruby locked her arm under hers as they walked side by side after the ceremony. She recalled feeling at that time as though nothing could tear them apart. Nothing.

Her grip tightened around the jacket before throwing it to the other side of the room and screaming out, "You fool! What were you thinking? Did you really expect her to love you as much as you loved her?" Only silence answered her. Even if someone had been in the room with her, no words could possibly be spoken to relieve the pain she felt inside.

She sat on the side of her bed next to her opened suitcase and released the sorrow that she'd hidden for so long. She glanced to the corner of the room where her favorite jacket lay. It was as crumpled and lifeless as she felt. Ella considered leaving it, and her past, behind. She knew her life would be much simpler without it, and her heart most certainly safer.

The minutes ticked by as she sat considering her fate and that of her trusty jacket. Soon her vision cleared, and she collected her valued belonging and dusted it off. She had no intention of packing it away with the rest of her clothing.

For fifteen minutes she looked at herself in the bathroom mirror, daring herself to do something she'd always wanted to do. She picked up a pair of scissors and felt the cold, heavy metal in her hand. As she gripped them tightly the metal began to warm and provided her comfort. Ella removed the ribbon that held her hair back and let her long locks fall loose around her shoulders. With her left hand she grabbed a fistful of hair, admiring how long it had become—almost to the middle of her back. Then, with a single snap of the scissors, she watched a clump of her thick, dark hair as it fell to the bathroom floor.

The scissors flashed with wild abandon; every cut liberated her from the person she pretended to be. She stopped and glanced quickly at her refection in the mirror before eagerly gathering two additional items from her suitcase. She returned with her hair pomade and her last remaining roll of heavy-duty cotton hospital gauze. The gauze had been given to her by one of the Red Cross nurses in Cora's group of friends, and effectively concealed her womanly traits.

With a handful of water, she slicked back her now-short hair, applied a liberal amount of pomade to keep every hair in place, and then wrapped the heavy gauze tightly around her chest. The bandage was so tight she could barely breathe, but it was a small price to pay for her liberation. Ella stood tall and breathed a sigh of relief. "There you are, Mr. O'Brien. I've been looking for you everywhere," he said with a pleased smile.

In the morning, Mr. O'Brien put on his best suit and tie, and stepped in front of the long mirror for the first time fully dressed as a gentleman. Looking at the image in the mirror, he was quite pleased to notice there was no longer any need to wear a hat to hide long hair. Lacking facial hair, O'Brien resembled a teenage boy rather than a thirty-four-year-old woman. Freedom was only a train ride away.

Any suitable gent at that time wore an appropriate hat when traveling. O'Brien held his favorite black bowler hat over his head as if it were a crown and eased it slowly down. Without the added hair, the hat fell below his ears. *That won't do.* He found two cotton handkerchiefs and folded them into the lining of the hat until the fit was just right, before heading to the train station. With a tap to the top of the felt bowler, Mr. O'Brien was on his way.

O'Brien could feel his heart racing as he passed through the large decorative door of the train station. *What if someone suspects I'm anything other than a young man traveling alone? What then?*

He pushed his fear aside and headed toward the old man sitting behind the ticket counter. The man was looking down at his newspaper with a day-old unlit cigar protruding from the left side of his mouth. O'Brien had arrived much earlier than the other travelers, and the ticket agent was clearly enjoying the solitude of the empty station.

Before taking one more step closer, he cleared his throat and settled his nerves. Ella's voice was naturally low, but this time Mr. O'Brien prayed it would be mannish enough. He walked with a long, boyish stride toward the ticket counter. The man glanced up from his newspaper to see who was approaching, and then quickly resumed his reading.

O'Brien was now standing at the counter. The old man continued reading, seeming unfazed by the presence of a customer. O'Brien cleared his throat again before speaking with the lowest voice he could muster. "Excuse me, my good sir. I'd like to purchase a ticket to Portland, Oregon."

The man looked up for only a moment, annoyed. "Listen kid, don't ya know that train doesn't leave for another three hours?"

O'Brien didn't budge. He stood there looking at the man without saying a word, until he put down his newspaper. With his cigar still firmly in his mouth, he said, "Oh all right, very well. Here's your ticket, son. Now beat it, will ya? Can't you see I'm busy?"

O'Brien passed the man the money and gathered his ticket. He smiled and gave a tip of the hat to the old man. "Good day, sir," he said. Even though he was annoyed by the man's rude behavior, the fact that he referred to O'Brien as "son" relieved him greatly.

Making his way to the train platform, O'Brien found an old newspaper to read. He watched as the other passengers started arriving, getting nervous again. After all, it was one thing to fool one cranky old man who probably couldn't see that well. It was quite another to pass in a crowd with so many people walking around him. This would be the real test.

O'Brien gathered his courage and his small bag, and headed toward the train. The steam trunk containing dresses had been left behind in the lobby of a hotel next to the station. There was no need for such things any longer.

In a rush to get to the train unnoticed, O'Brien stumbled into a man standing on the platform. The impact was so hard the man almost fell to his knees. The man turned around and stood face to face with Mr. O'Brien, who was stunned and unsure what the man would do until he complained, "Say, buddy, what's the big idea? Watch where you're going, why don't you?"

After apologizing to the man, O'Brien tipped his hat and moved aside to allow him and his wife to board the train. Before stepping up to enter the train, Mr. O'Brien turned around and looked up into the rust-colored clouds above, taking in one last breath of Wisconsin air before boarding.

As the speed of the train increased and it got farther from town, he could feel the rhythmic pounding in his chest and imagined it was his heart starting to beat again. Mr. O'Brien looked into his reflection in the window and settled into the long journey to Oregon.

The empty seat next to him was a reminder that love is not always about forever. Sometimes it is simply about knowing that love is possible. Heading to Portland without his beloved was different this time—this time he was leaving on his own terms, and finally felt freedom.

Ella as Mr. O'Brien

FIFTY-FIVE

July 1, 1921

Ruby had never felt so alone. With her wedding to Arnold less than two months away, the darkness of her thoughts was threatening to swallow her whole. She knew Ella had already started her new life in Portland, and any hope they would ever honor their wedding vows was gone. Deep down, she prayed Ella would somehow appear at her door and take her away from darkness to light.

As Ruby sat in the murkiness of her room, she heard a knock at the door. She peered down from her window and saw what looked to be a young gentleman standing on the front porch. He was wearing the same type of suit and bowler hat Ella would wear. Her heart pounded as she ran down the stairs, thinking her prayers had been answered. *She came back for me,* she thought.

She flung open the door and a nervous young man quickly removed his hat. "Excuse me, ma'am, my name is Walter Thomas. I hate to be a bother, but my father, William Thomas, told me to come over here and talk with Mr. Peterson about a job. Is Mr. Peterson home?"

Her romantic notion of finding Ella standing on her porch dashed, Ruby was left speechless in the doorway, unable to react to the young man's question. For what seemed to be an eternity she stood there, staring at him and trying to regain her breath.

She felt her body shaking from the inside as her world spun out of control. Ruby began screaming at Walter, "Who are you? What are you doing here? Where is Ella?"

Walter, now more frightened than nervous, apologized. "Ma-ma'am, I'm sorry! My name is Walter Thomas, and my..."

Ruby interrupted Walter's well-rehearsed speech. "I don't care who you are or why you're here. Do you hear me? You get off my property now or I'll call the police."

With his hat in hand, Walter was already halfway down the street, running toward town, by the time Ruby stepped back inside the safety of her home. When she closed the door behind her she fell to her knees and started to pray. "Dear God, please help me. I'm not strong enough to do this alone. My heart is weak and I'm not sure how much more I can take. Please God, help me!"

By the time Ruby's father came home that evening he had already heard about what happened at his home that day. The Thomas boy was telling everyone in town how crazy Ruby was acting. When Peter Peterson walked in his house he headed directly for the phone. He knew talking to Ruby about what had happened would be pointless; the only person able to reason with her was Ada.

FIFTY-SIX

When Ada arrived four days later, her father told her that Ruby had not taken one step outside her room since the Thomas boy was there. Not even for food or water. Ada was beside herself. "Father, why in the world would you not bring her anything to eat or drink?"

Her father scratched the back of his head, searching for an answer, but he seemed just as perplexed as Ada. "I don't know. I reckoned if she got hungry enough she would come out eventually. Besides, she's going to be twenty-five years old in a few weeks. Why do I have to take care of her like she's a child?"

When Ada opened Ruby's bedroom door there was only a small stream of light trickling in from outside. Ruby had covered all her windows with thick wool blankets to keep the sunlight and the world at bay. Ada stood in the doorway, waiting for her eyes to adjust, before walking into the darkness. There was no sound from Ruby, and she could barely see the outline of her sister lying in bed. The air was musty and thick with despair. As she walked over to a window to remove one of the blankets, she called out, "Ruby, how are you feeling? Papa tells me you nearly scared the Thompson boy to death. The whole town is talking about how crazy you are. Honestly, Ruby, I've never known anyone to be so upset about getting married."

Ada froze when she realized there was no answer or movement from her sister. She softly called out again, "Ruby, are you all right?"

There was no response.

Ada could feel her heart pounding. She didn't dare to think why her sister wasn't responding. She called out again, this time much louder, "Ruby Sarah Peterson. Are you all right? Answer me!"

Still nothing.

Ada now feared she had arrived too late. She ran to the side of the bed, pulled back the covers, and screamed out Ruby's name one more time. As she did, Ruby reached up with her hands to shield her eyes from the sunlight now streaming in. Ada was relieved to see movement from her sister; however, without food or water for days, Ruby was a shell of herself. A soft whisper of words came from Ruby, which Ada struggled to understand. She knelt down by the side of the bed and heard Ruby saying in a faint whisper, "Ada, please stop. I've got the worst headache, and you mustn't scream at me like that. Just leave me alone so I can die in peace."

"My God, Ruby! What in the world has happened? I've never seen you like this before."

Ada was expecting another whispered response from her sister, but Ruby had fallen unconscious. Ada began shaking her and calling out, "Papa! Please come here quickly! There is something terribly wrong with Ruby."

By the time their father reached Ruby's bedside, Ruby was starting to regain consciousness. He stood in silence, staring down at his youngest daughter for a moment before the gravity of the situation took hold and he reached for Ruby's hand. "Why would you do such a thing, my child? Please don't be like this. I love you and only want what's best for you."

With all of the energy Ruby had, she said, "I know, Daddy. I'm just not sure I'm strong enough to make you happy."

Ada returned to the room with a big glass of water and some food; she forced Ruby to drink and take small bites of cheese. Her father sat on the bed next to Ruby to make sure she was eating and drinking. However, every couple of bites she would gag on the food and threaten to stop eating. "I can't do this. I don't want to do this. Can't you both please leave me alone?"

Ada turned to her father for answers. "Why is she acting this way? Will she be all right?" Their father was just as confused about what was happening. He had no answers.

Ada began frantically searching for something in Ruby's closet, finally pulling out a light-blue dress. "We need to get her to the hospital in Stevens Point, I know a nurse there who can help us. There's a train leaving in fifteen minutes and we must get there in time. Come on, Ruby. Let's get you to the doctor. Daddy, help me get her dressed."

The three of them arrived at the train station with only minutes to spare. With the little food and water Ruby had been able to keep down she had enough energy to walk, but still needed assistance. Ada decided it would be best if only she and Ruby traveled to the Stevens Point Hospital. If anyone asked what was wrong with Ruby, she would tell them she was suffering from 'female problems'—a subject nobody ever wanted to talk about.

FIFTY-SEVEN

While Ruby and Ada were sitting in the hospital waiting room, a familiar nurse walked by. She was wearing a gray dress, a crisp white apron, and a heavily starched nurse's hat with a red cross on the front. Ada quickly recognized her from one of Cora's parties a few years earlier, and politely called out, "Excuse me, Harriet, can you please help me with my sister?"

Harriet didn't recognize Ada right away, but then quickly realized how she knew Ruby. At first she panicked, fearing her outside life would be revealed, but seeing Ruby's condition she realized there was a serious situation at hand. "My god! Is that Ruby? What in the world happened to her?"

Before Ada could respond, Harriet reached for Ruby's hand. "There's no time to waste. Help me get her to her feet. I'll take her back to see a doctor immediately."

Ruby glanced over her shoulder at Ada one more time for reassurance as Harriet led her down the long, sterile gray hallway. Ada looked into her sister's eyes and nodded to let her know everything would be fine, but deep down she wasn't sure that was true. She noticed how frail her sister seemed and how unsure her footsteps were even with Harriet's assistance. She wondered if somehow she could have done something to prevent what Ruby was going through.

Ruby woke up to the sound of a woman screaming and thought she was having a horrible nightmare. Her body felt heavy and her mind was foggy. She could hear people talking outside her door and the sound of footsteps walking away. Looking around the gray, pictureless walls, she struggled to make sense of it all.

Glancing up, she saw a glass of water on the table next to the bed. She reached for it, but found she was unable to raise her right arm. The woman in the next room screamed again, and Ruby panicked. She looked down to find heavy leather straps attached to each of her wrists and tightly bound on either side of the bed. She pulled on the straps, hoping to break free, but to no avail.

She screamed out for help, but nobody came. Fear and adrenaline filled her body, and she started pulling even harder on the restraints. The leather dug through the skin on her right wrist and a trickle of dark red blood flowed down her arm. The leather became slippery with blood, and she could feel her hand starting to slip from its bondage.

Ruby was about to pull her hand free when she heard the echo of footsteps coming down the hall toward her. The footsteps stopped at her door and a key entered the lock. By the time the tumblers on the lock turned and the door opened, Ruby had assumed her original position in bed and was trying to hide her partially freed hand.

A nurse stepped in and Ruby called out, "Harriet, thank God you're here! They've got me tied up to this bed. Please hurry up and free me so I can get out of here."

Before closing the door behind her, Harriet looked down the hall to make sure none of the doctors or other nurses had seen her enter Ruby's room. "Ruby, you must keep your voice down. I'm not supposed to be in a patient's room alone."

"Patient? I'm not a patient. I'm not sick. I had a headache for a couple of days, but that's no reason for me to be tied to a bed all day like a prisoner of war."

Harriet was desperate. "Ruby, please quiet your voice. A doctor will be coming to your room any minute and I've got to talk with you before he gets here. You must listen to me very carefully. First of all, you've been a patient at the hospital for the last five days. They've been treating you for hysteria and giving you drugs to keep you asleep. I work on this floor, and I'll help you, but only if you don't tell anyone you know me, or anything about me. Ruby, do you understand?"

Ruby was shocked to find out she had been there for five days. "But Harriet, I'm not sick or crazy. You know I'm not."

"No, Ruby, you're not sick or crazy. None of us are. But we are all prisoners of this war. If anyone outside our group found out that the boys we're with are not actually boys, they'd lock us all away. What you need to decide, Ruby Peterson, is if you are going to be a prisoner who lives in a cage or outside of one."

Harriet held her breath, waiting for Ruby to decide if her secret would be kept. Apart from the screaming of the woman next door, there was silence in the room. Harriet looked down and saw the trail of blood on Ruby's bedding and followed it to her arm. "Heavens, Ruby, don't you know if you try to escape they're only going to give you more sleeping pills. Or worse, give you a shot of malaria to sweat the sickness out of your head."

Just as Harriet was starting to wipe the blood away from Ruby's arm the door opened and Dr. White walked into the room. "Nurse, what are you doing in here alone with this patient?"

Harriet's face was flushed as she quickly searched for a suitable response for the doctor. "It's my fault, doctor," Ruby said. "You see, I have always had terrible night dreams and I must have accidentally cut myself on the side of the bed."

As Ruby was explaining her wound to the doctor, Harriet knew she would keep her secret. "Yes, doctor, I was just going to call for you right before you came in."

The doctor looked at Ruby's hand and seemed satisfied with the explanation given. "Very well, then. The cut doesn't look like it needs stitches. Nurse, clean up this mess while I review Miss Peterson's chart."

With a silent nod of acceptance between them, Harriet wrapped Ruby's injury in white cotton gauze. Ruby understood that even though her beloved wife was gone, she was unwilling to surrender her life to the gray walls that surrounded her.

∽◦!◦∾

My Grandma Ruby never forgot what it felt like to be held down by those leather straps, unable to move because someone had decided it was the best thing for her. Maybe that's why later in life she felt compelled to release patients in the retirement home when they asked her to. I believe I would have done the same thing under the circumstances.

FIFTY-EIGHT

It was the night before her wedding to Arnold. Ruby was still taking the pills the doctors had given her to settle her nerves. She couldn't remember how many pills she had already taken that day, but decided one more wouldn't hurt.

The last pill was starting to take effect and her eyes began to lose focus. She was hardly able to hold the pencil in her hand. However, in her last few hours of freedom, she decided to write to her pals to say her final goodbyes.

There were five letters or poems written by my Grandma Ruby the night before her marriage to Arnold Anderson. I was able to transcribe all of them except for her fifth; I believe the full effect of the medication she was given by the doctor left her unable to complete her final letter in any legible manner. No edits or corrections were made to the four letters transcribed below.

Letter One:

> *Goodbye Pals I'm going far away.*
> *This duty calls me and I am leaving*
> *I fear I'll leave them all aggrieving*
> *goodbye and give my love*
> *to Maude and France*

and all of the girls I know.
Just like a soldier boy I
bring into this strife
a battle for my life.

Letter Two:

Goodbye old Pals
I'll be faithful for she says you.
I'll come right back
with no.
If she should fight
and make a scene
I'll take the next train
out to Racine.
Goodbye and if alive
and well next year.
I'll surely meet you here
if not remember I did fight
for my rights
My rights to say our rights.

Letter Three:

Goodbye Boys I'm
Going to get married tomorrow
I'm going from sunshine to
Sorrow
No more waiting at the old
States door

No more roving on the ocean

Shore

I believe I must forget

So goodbye boys.

Letter Four:

Goodnight nurse tell the

doctor I'm no better

Write my folks a nice

long letter.

Say I need a rest with you

I might be better if I stay here

a year.

Feel my pulse hold my

hand a little longer

how's my heart don't you

think it's getting stronger.

Tell me in the morning or

I'll get worse.

Kiss your little patient

Goodnight nurse.

FIFTY-NINE

August 21, 1921

There was a flood of excitement in the Peterson home on the morning of Ruby's and Arnold's wedding. Many relatives from Stevens Point, Milwaukee, and Minneapolis had taken the train into Amherst in the last few days to help decorate the home.

As more and more people arrived, Ruby felt her loneliness growing deeper. Most people figured Ruby was held up in her room getting ready for her 'big day' like most brides do. She could hear them all laughing and talking outside her room as they hung white and yellow ribbons and bows around the home. The noise was pushing in from every direction as she sat on the side of her bed, not sure if she could to go through with it. She told herself over and over again that if others before her had done it, she could too.

Besides, with all the people showing up, there would be no escaping without embarrassing both families and Arnold, and she knew it wasn't Arnold's fault. He'd be just as willing to forget the whole wedding as she was.

When she heard the train going by she considered bolting out her second-floor window, running toward it as fast as she could, and jumping on board. For the first time in her life she hated the sound of the train. After so many years of dreaming about all the wonderful places it would take her, it now seemed to snicker and taunt her as it rolled past her house, its famous whistle screaming louder, knowing she wanted to leave but was trapped. She heard the train passing on the bridge down the street and covered her ears with her hands, hoping it would stop calling her name—hoping everything would just stop, and all the people gathered outside her door would go away.

When she slowly removed her hands from the sides of her head, all she could hear were the sounds of furniture in the house being moved around to make way for more people. Her head was still pounding, even though she had taken the pills the doctor prescribed the day before. Ruby asked herself, *My God, when will they stop making all that noise? Why are so many people here to watch this farce of a wedding? I'm sure most of them are here for the free food, or to gossip.* Ruby laughed out loud. *At least they'll have one less thing to gossip about after today.*

Ada slowly opened the door to Ruby's bedroom. She could tell by the look on Ruby's face that she was frightened and wanted to run away. Ada's job was to make sure Ruby made it down the aisle toward her new husband, and that's what she was going to do.

"Come on sister, this is a wedding, not a funeral. Please try to put on a happy face, won't you?"

"How am I to do that, Ada? When you and Charles got married you at least liked each other and you both wanted the same things. You gave up your teaching to become a wife and mother because that's what you wanted. However, I don't want that, and neither does Arnold. He's just as scared as I am. What kind of marriage will this be for either of us?"

"Ruby, none of us really know how marriage will work out, but you've got to try. If you don't, I— " Ada stopped herself.

"What, Ada? Just say it. You don't know what will become of me? Is that what you were going to say?"

"No. I was going to say that if you don't, I'm not sure what Papa will do. He blames himself for you not wanting to get married. He thinks if he was a better father to you after Mama passed, you would be, well, like the rest of us."

"But Ada, it's not his fault, or Mama's. It's not your fault or mine. I haven't found the right fellow yet, that's all. I just need more time."

"Ruby, please stop. We both know that's not true. You've had plenty of handsome gentlemen after you, and any one of them would have been a perfectly good husband. I know you love Ella. I was there, remember? I was there when you and Ella got married. I know what I saw. At first I thought it was something you were doing just to be funny. You can lie to Papa and the others, but not to me. Ruby, you have to know that the life you want with Ella, or any woman, is not natural. I'm afraid if you don't go through with this wedding with Arnold you will live a lifetime of pain and shame. Not only for yourself, but the family as well."

Ruby watched as her sister started to cry and knew then what had to be done. She took a deep breath of air and swallowed every bit of courage she had. She opened the drawer to her dressing table and found her mother's perfume bottle, which now contained only a few good drops of rosewater. She applied the last remaining drops to her wrist and threw the empty bottle in the trash. Ruby reached for the large bouquet of white and yellow roses that was sitting on her dressing table. As she picked them up, she locked her hand underneath Ada's arm for support and said, "Come on sister, let's get this wedding over with."

SIXTY

On my list of things to see and do in Wisconsin on June 9, 2015, was find-ing Ella's grave. The day after going to the site of Ruby and Ella's wedding, I took a short drive from Amherst to the cemetery where Ella was buried. It was a small cemetery, so I knew finding her would not be as difficult as finding the others. By this time, I considered myself proficient in locating relatives who had long since passed and been forgotten.

Driving with my windows down, I could smell the fields and pas-tures as I passed farm after farm. Waves of different scents traveled through the air, changing from fields of grass to the sweet smell of dirt, then to woodlands. While I was there, I often drove with my windows down, even if it was raining. The spring rain added another layer of aroma that I wished I could bottle and bring back home with me.

As my GPS guided me to the cemetery through wide-open fields, I could tell I was getting closer. Soon I saw my destination ahead. It seemed like such a strange location for a cemetery—in the middle of nowhere, really. There was only one house, located across the street from it. Other than the dog barking at me from that house and the squawking of a single crow overhead, there was no sound.

As I searched for Ella's headstone I couldn't help but once again notice the rolling hills of farmland as far as I could see. As I looked up to admire the beautiful surroundings, I heard—and felt—a low-pitched vibration. The sound went through me, breaking the solitude, as I looked around for its source. It didn't seem to be man-made. At first I thought it was a far-away thunderstorm, but there were no clouds above me or on the horizon. I considered that it might be a high-flying airplane, train, or humming from phone or electrical lines, though there were no visible signs of any of these. I told myself there must be a reasonable explanation, and prepared to resume my search.

Before I could take one more step, I looked down and there she was: 'Daughter - Ella Karnopp 1886-1948.' I was so engrossed with the view around me that I had almost walked by her. The mysterious sound suddenly stopped, leaving only the rustling of a light breeze blowing through the trees and the happy chirping of birds above me. I stood at her gravesite, looking down at the long-lost friend I had never met.

I felt the sting of tears in my eyes as I knelt down to greet her and to wipe the dust from her name. The grounds around her were well-maintained, but I still felt compelled to remove some of the overgrown weeds. By this time, that had become one of my rituals when visiting long-lost relatives and friends.

I brought a small bouquet of silk daisies to be placed at her headstone; I didn't think Ella would like anything very fancy or flowery. As I knelt down again to secure the flowers into the ground, the strangest thing happened. The back of my head started tingling, and suddenly I envisioned my grandmother's hands adjusting Ella's boutonniere just like she might have done on their wedding day. My hands had somehow become my grandmother's hands, and for that moment Ella and Ruby reconnected.

After the sensation passed, I stood there for a couple of minutes to re-center myself in reality. At first I was confused about what had just happened to me, but then I sensed a feeling of contentment, as if the circle of love that had been left open for so many years was now completed and whole again. For that moment, Ruby and Ella were again married to each other.

Ella continued her teaching career at Jefferson High School as a history and English teacher until she retired in 1946. It's still unknown to me if she ever found love on the West Coast. However, I do know her last name never changed, which indicates she never entered into a conventional marriage. I can only hope she did find love again before her death on March 15, 1948.

Only in death did she return to her hometown in Almond, Wisconsin. Her body was brought back by train to be placed in the family plot in that small cemetery outside of town, next to her mother and father.

EPILOGUE

On June 27, 2015, I cried tears of joy along with thousands of others when the Supreme Court ruled it unconstitutional to refuse us the right to marry. On that day I rejoiced for me, my Grandma Ruby and Ella, and the millions of people who had come before us and sacrificed so much.

The fact does not elude me that if Grandma Ruby had been able to live the life she wanted with Ella, I would not be here today. However, I am also a firm believer in fate. I believe one of the reasons I'm here was to find my grandmother's photos and to tell her story. She had the courage to keep the photos as a reminder that love is possible even in an impossible time.

I can now stand outside of the shadows and proudly embrace my wife, openly sharing my life with the woman I love.

VARIOUS PHOTOS

Photos of Sara and Bessie taken around 1916

Bessie and Sara Yesterday and Today

Sara as Martha Washington, Bessie as a Solder

Unknown Women   *Darkie & Ruby as Pete*

Unknown Men (Idle Guys)

Unknown Man Wearing Bloomers

DON'T YOU DARE

Maud and Frances

Leroy and Foxy 1915

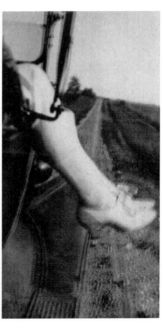

Ruby, Leroy and Ada
Just home from the fair (1920)

Ruby heading home

Various Photos – Not for duplication – All rights received

Acknowledgments

I am deeply grateful to the following people for their assistance, words of encouragement, and inspiration: Kim Lewis, Davina Kotulski, Johnny Silva Schaefer, Janice Fusillo, Deirdre DiBiaggio, Katie Carmichael, Meredith Taylor, Gay Kinman, Cynthia Naden, Merlin Turner, Bill Turner, Rianna Scipio, Nancy Kehr, Sue Fitzmaurice, Denise Michel, Stephanie Gunning, Bob Rausch, Tom Ashline, and the beautiful town of Amherst, Wisconsin.